TEEN SPIRIT

Sparking
CONNECTION WITH
YOUR **TEENAGER**

PRAGATI JALAN SUREKA

HAY HOUSE

HAY HOUSE INDIA
New Delhi • London • Sydney
Carlsbad, California • New York City

Hay House Publishers (India) Pvt Ltd,
Muskaan Complex, Plot No. 3, B-2, Vasant Kunj, New Delhi 110 070, India
Hay House LLC, P.O. Box 5100, Carlsbad, CA 92018-5100, USA
Hay House UK Ltd, The Sixth Floor, Watson House, 54 Baker Street, London W1U 7BU, UK
Hay House Australia Publishing Pty Ltd, 18/36 Ralph St., Alexandria NSW 2015, Australia

Email: contact@hayhouse.co.in
www.hayhouse.co.in

ISBN 978-81-19554-99-7
ISBN 978-81-19554-71-3 (Ebook)

Printed at
Thomson Press India Limited

FSC
www.fsc.org
MIX
Paper | Supporting responsible forestry
FSC® C010615

'The intriguing mechanics of a teenage mind have kept the world on the edge ever since. Something changes, a tide turns, a wind shifts, the moment a human body becomes teen years old. More importantly, a crucial conversation is prematurely ended. Pragati's book is about that inevitable crucial conversation that never happened—the conversation between teenagers and their parents. It is a nudge to initiate that essential communication. With its quizzes, first-person anecdotes narrated by teenagers, professional recommendations, and emphasis on the importance of open, honest dialogue, *Teen Spirit* provides a roadmap for creating a supportive environment that nurtures the mental health of teenagers. Every parent, and teenager, must know about this book, own it, and read it.'

—Shruti Kohli
Author of *The Petticoat Journal*

'If you are struggling to understand and connect with your teenage child, *Teen Spirit* provides hope. Pragati's research-backed book sheds light on what so many of us struggle with and provides insight into how we can overcome these challenges. This book helps us understand what is happening during this developmental period and provides concrete strategies and tools that help us navigate this developmental stage to ensure that we have a lifelong healthy relationship with our children. Pragati shows us how our children can be our best teachers if we choose to see and listen to them.'

—Monica Hughson
Founder and CEO of Full-Purpose Coaching

'*Teen Spirit* is the definite winner in the parenting guidebook. Its firmament standing as a sourcebook of useful hints spiked with real-life experiences. The best choice for its easy-to-understand step-by-step terms and practical expert advice.'

—Dr Parijat Das
Department of Microbiology, Tata Medical Centre

'It is a must-read book to guide parents in traversing this tricky journey of parenting teens. A definitive guide to meaningful relationships, understanding the world of your teenager, and effective strategies to parent them with profound insights and pragmatic advice are what this book stands to offer. *Teen Spirit* is a silver lining for parents who want to make a difference in the lives of their teenagers.'

—Ashutosh Garg
Author and Founder of The Brand Called You

'This book is useful in learning, concisely and succinctly—how to understand teen's mindsets and problems. A lot of low-hanging fruit is available for us to pluck from these passages and get connected with our teenage children. Relationships which will make our and our teenagers' lives so much more meaningful.'

—Rahul Pasari
Director, Assam Roofing Limited

For anyone who has ever questioned their abilities as a parent, let this book be a guiding light of comfort and encouragement.

Contents

Introduction 9

1. The Parenting Experience 11
2. Enhancing Adolescent Well-Being 29
3. Mapping Our Bonds: Recognising the Internal Dynamics of Connection 41
4. What Is Effective Parenting? 49
5. Building Rituals and Creating Spaces for Open Dialogue 65
6. Parenting with Love 73
7. Managing Parental Irritability 79
8. Cognitive Behavioural Therapy to Improve Parent-Teen Communication 85
9. Life Transitions: A Guide for Teens 91
10. Nurturing Autonomy and Emotional Health in Teenagers 101
11. Harnessing the Power of Humility 117
12. Unmasking the Harmful Effects of Toxic Positivity 123
13. Unlocking Adolescent Self-Sabotage 131

14. Parental Burnout: Consequences and Coping Strategies 141

15. The Art of Persuasion 155

16. Supporting Teens through Stress and Unexpected Challenges 163

17. Parenting with Compassionate Love 173

18. Exploring the Essence of a Good Parent-Teen Relationship 185

19. Parenting Master Key: Repair Attempts 197

20. Healthy Strategies for Connecting with Your Teen 209

21. Love: The Ultimate Force 217

Afterword 229

Acknowledgements 231

Bibliography 232

Introduction

Parenting requires a manual. Gender stereotyping, societal expectations, and one's own early childhood experiences all influence each individual's parenting style. While there is much emphasis on attachment styles, adverse situations, and the type of parenting one receives, there is rarely a solution-focused approach to parenting that acknowledges that two plus two will equal four, regardless of past experiences and beliefs.

This may sound too good to be true, but it's not. It's quite simple. There are certain universal challenges that every parent faces, causing them to doubt their competence, particularly when dealing with teenagers. In this book, we will embark on a journey of parenting teenagers together.

What are the skills of healthy and effective parenting? Psychologists assert that individuation, or the ability to survive and live independently, is the desired goal for all adults. Therefore, it naturally follows that independent thinking, indicated by one's viewpoint, self-control, freedom, autonomy, and role modelling of desirable skills, is the preferred approach to healthy parenting.

When parents constantly 'tell' a child what to do, how it would be 'good' for them, and judge their worth based on compliance, it sabotages and undermines healthy relationships between parents and their adolescents. No one likes feeling controlled by another, especially not your teenager.

One of the main reasons that I decided to write on this topic is to provide simple, engaging, and specific information on parenting. The knowledge in this book is based on concrete, well-researched concepts. Furthermore, it was important to have a specific parenting book for parenting teenagers, which did not shy away from taking the bull by the horns. The hope was to write based on real case studies and demonstrate how difficult theoretical concepts can be presented as an easy read and are relatable. The chapters are set in an easy, effective, sustainable, and usable format.

Parents often get overwhelmed by simple developmental stages and behaviours. One common example is an adolescent child's increasing need for physical distancing and less communication with parents. Adolescence is a time of turbulent transformation.

Awareness of issues, whether physical or emotional, helps in being prepared for them, especially for parenting. While physical changes associated with puberty, like thickening of voice in boys, sprouting of beard, menarche, etc., are something that most parents are aware of, there is a dearth of information about what the emotional challenges that adolescents face and how they can cope with them. Parents rarely know that they are unaware of the basic issues that all adolescents face. Most of them have forgotten their struggles as teenagers. There is a comforting patina of complacency for their own bygone difficult teenage years. They tend to minimise problems that children voice, saying, 'It is no big deal; we also faced it.'

This book specifically shows parents how to understand, communicate, and cope with their child's mental and emotional changes.

1

The Parenting Experience

'To Parent Perfectly is a mirage. There is no ideal parent and no ideal child.'

—Dr Shefali Tsabary

Our parenting experience can be profoundly enriching if done skilfully. It may sound too good to be true, but it actually isn't. As the saying goes, 'The journey of a million miles begins with a single step.' Your journey as a healthy parent begins now.

Often, our perception of ourselves as parents of teenagers is based on fantasies of cosy chats, trips together, and bonding over movies. We believe that our purse strings, values, beliefs, hopes, aspirations, and experiences automatically make us loving, supportive, and involved parents. We are so entrenched in our own vision and of being the 'best'—indulgent, nurturing, and supportive—that we rarely pause to consider our child's experience of us as their parent.

We are so certain that we can never majorly err that we often unconsciously, and sometimes even consciously, blame our children when communication issues arise with our teenagers. We forget a fundamental truth: Children have their own viewpoint, which may differ from ours. Each of us must use our own mind for our own thinking, just as each of us must live in our own body and not in anyone else's.

Even when we realise that we may not be as approachable to our teenagers as we think, we tend to ignore this uncomfortable truth and cling to what we want to believe—that we know what is best for our teens.

All Parents are Loving Parents

But do our teenagers perceive us as such? Let's explore what a young 19-year-old shared with me when asked about the challenges she faced in relating to her parents.

> Name: Ankita Sethia
> Gender: Female (she/her/hers)
> Age: 19
> Family Type: Joint

> One of the earliest instances I recall where I couldn't confide in my parents was about having friendships with the opposite gender. Attending an all-girls school, introducing the idea of being friends with a boy was challenging. It felt unfamiliar, and having a male friend seemed significant. It was often perceived as romantic, and fearing misinterpretation, I refrained from discussing these friendships with my parents.
>
> The generational gap, coupled with the belief that boys and girls can never simply be friends, further complicated matters. Understanding that we belong to a different generation and shouldn't be treated exactly as our parents were treated is difficult for them. While it may seem straightforward to acknowledge and sympathise with this perspective, over time, it has affected my relationship with my parents.

Another sensitive topic to broach has been sex, particularly concerning teen pregnancy. The notion that virginity is merely a social construct and doesn't signify 'purity' as commonly portrayed is challenging to address. If left unaddressed, it can lead to issues for a child. Often, children end up learning about these topics elsewhere before the conversation takes place. This discussion also encompasses the LGBTQIA+ community. The stigma attached to being gay can damage self-identity. The conversation sometimes devolves into questioning one's identity and sexuality, or it's expressed that the parents would be disappointed if their child wasn't heterosexual.

The neglect of mental health is another significant issue. The concept of burnout or the fact that today's younger generation faces more pressures than their parents did at the same age is difficult for parents to comprehend. This misconception leads to mental health being dismissed or deemed unimportant, as continuous pressure and hard work are seen as the sole paths to success.

Being from a different generation, pressuring children to pursue conventional career paths poses another challenge. Parents often lack awareness about emerging fields and may discourage children from pursuing paths they genuinely enjoy. The common expectation of becoming an engineer or doctor is deeply ingrained in some parents' minds and initially caused difficulties for me. I do not feel loved by them.

Whether we are prepared to acknowledge it or not, our children often feel pressured due to our dysfunctional and dogmatic ideas, values, beliefs, and preconceptions. When pressurised, they do not feel loved by parents.

Parenting Is a Reflection of Our Intrapersonal Relationship

Every relationship we have reflects our relationship with ourselves and how we perceive ourselves. We are rarely able to accept ourselves, as we tend to innately doubt our own self-worth because of so-called faults within. We rarely accept all sides of our personality, especially traits that we feel are not very socially celebrated. So, to begin the journey of parenting smoothly, it is important to stop being so disconnected from our own feelings and emotions.

Think of a time when you were struggling to communicate with your child. Now, rather than focusing on what the incident was and how they were to blame, take a step back and observe your own self at that point. Were you mentally prepared to have that difficult conversation at that time? Were you calm and collected? Were you completely present during the communication? Were you constantly distracted by phone calls or other things? Were you multitasking too much at that time? Were you stressed at work? Were you concerned about health or something else? Were you facing challenges related to sleep? Were you physically exhausted or mentally drained?

If you answered no to more than two of these questions, it indicates your emotional unavailability at that point. When we are unavailable, we are not in the frame of mind to pay attention. We seem in a hurry to finish our point of view without truly having the bandwidth to explore how our words are impacting them. Furthermore, we miss the opportunity to pick up helpful cues from our child's body language, which could potentially improve our communication.

When we attend an important meeting, we are usually committed in terms of time, attention, and focus. We tend to be well-prepared with facts, our strengths, weaknesses, and contributions about how we can be of help. Yet, when it comes to talking to children, we often find ourselves distracted and, if we're honest, a little nonchalant. We are not adequately prepared for successful and effective conversations with children. Consider this: If we really pay attention, we will remember the principle of HALT, which means refraining from important conversations when we are hungry, angry, late, or tired.

Whether we admit or not, the reason we face challenges communicating with our adolescents is because we have a preconceived mindset that 'they won't listen, so there's no point in talking.' As parents, we are often emotionally unavailable when speaking to them. We may be busy checking our phones, running late for social engagements or work meeting, or simply caught up in adult responsibilities. Let's be honest—we all have plenty of experience 'adulting'. However, when it comes to parenting, we sometimes forget to be compassionate towards children and expect them to navigate adult challenges effortlessly.

The reason we struggle to understand others, especially children, is because at some level, we are unwilling to understand ourselves. We have been criticised incessantly about our flaws, work ethic, or how we don't measure up to others. This criticism, whether acknowledged or not, influences our behaviour. We tend to focus on what's lacking, and in this mindset, one aspect that suffers is parenting and communication. We are so focused on meeting our needs as parents that we overlook what the child needs. Our fearful attitude about a child's success in life stems from our own deep-rooted fears instilled by our own parents.

To be a healthy parent, we must first acknowledge those hurts, rejections, fears, and disapprovals lying unprocessed within ourselves, which make us bristly and fearful as parents.

So, are any of these thoughts or questions racing through your mind right now?

> How do I process it?
>
> How do I improve myself as a parent?
>
> How do I free myself from this vicious cycle of hurt, fear, and disapproval?

Do not worry if you do not know 'how'. Read on to find the answers to these questions and many more concepts that will be useful. Whether we are aware or not of how we relate to our own children is determined, largely, by our relationship blueprint from our childhood. Even two children born as siblings in the same home to the same parents tend to have different relationship blueprints based on their gender, age of parents when they were born, parental difficulties at their birth, and own birth order (i.e., whether they are first born, middle born, youngest, or only child). Sometimes, if the family is facing a financial crunch, health issues, bereavement, or any other issue, the age at which the child experiences those challenges and the state of the parents' own emotional state and availability form a part of this blueprint and show the impact of those early relationship dynamics throughout life.

Melanie Klein delves into this concept extensively within her 'Object Relations Theory' where she elucidates how we inherit our relationship blueprints from our parents and how we perceive the treatment we received from them. The desire for affectionate, warm, and fun relationships with our children in universal. We want their admiration and love, yet when faced with an indifferent expression, it's often challenging to accept our potential role in its development. Instead, we tend to attribute such difficulties to external factors such as media influence, peer pressure, or societal norms, thereby absolving ourselves of personal responsibility.

However, what if we take firm hold of the nettle? What if we entertain the notion that, perhaps, the root of relational dysfunction lies within our own parenting skills? While this realisation may initially sting, it also presents a silver lining. By acknowledging our own contributions to the dynamics of our relationships, we reclaim agency over the situation. Rather than feeling at the mercy of our rebellious teenagers, we empower ourselves to effect positive change. Does this new perspective not fill you with hope?

The good news is that we can become skilled at creating healthy relationships with our children by revisiting our own childhood traumas. Talking about our difficulties in childhood and courageously owning up to how we struggled will help us become more empathetic to what our children are going through. While outwardly they may seem to have more materialistic gains than we did, their emotional vacuum is often much larger than we can imagine.

When we process our emotional journey up to this point by answering the questions interspersed throughout this book, we can introspect and tap into the power of our innate emotional intelligence by embarking on a path of self-awareness. By shining a ray of awareness into our own pains, rejections, and difficulties while growing up, we can grieve, let go, and ultimately heal from those repressed emotions, traumas, patterns, and incidents.

Even when it is painful to revisit seemingly forgotten, old, and hurtful childhood memories, it is important to do so. The reason is simple: Mary Ainsworth's research shows us that we recreate the same difficult dynamics of our own childhood in our parenting journey. If we have a history of being emotionally ignored, especially as teenagers, we cannot help but repeat the same pattern with our own children. If our parents expected us to follow instructions blindly as adolescents, somewhere in our heart lies a secret wish for the same from our children, even if we feel ashamed to admit it as 'modern' parents (Ainsworth et al. 1978). As relationship coach Alan Robarge says, 'We perpetuate our dysfunction when we do not address this old blueprint.'

The Role of Education

In our early years, education is presented as the primary pursuit. We are often told that the key to a successful, happy, and fulfilling adult life lies in our formative education. Consequently, we are taught and pressured to maintain good grades, regardless of difficulties, interests, or capabilities. Yet, one must consider the toll this external focus takes on the emotional well-being of growing adolescents. Today, suicide rates, youth violence, and psychopathology in teens are at an all-time high. Public healthcare systems, as well as global mental health initiatives, are strained due to a shortage of trained psychologists and mental healthcare workers. Demand exceeds the supply of helping professionals. In such a climate, it is crucial to emphasise the prevention of mental health issues by promoting stability at home conducive to the emotional well-being of all family members. Therefore, it is imperative that healthy parenting and a warm, nurturing, and loving atmosphere become the norm across households rather than a desirable but utopian concept.

Childhood is complex. Yet, many people tend to view their own childhood through rose-tinted glasses or deny the realities of what truly occurred. Our internal scripts, beliefs, and patterns of behaviour are established in childhood. Our success as parents greatly depends on how we perceive our own childhood. Our attitudes toward relationships, strangers, or friends are determined during childhood.

While there is significant emphasis on external education, there is often little focus on internal education, which entails understanding and accepting our own minds, thoughts, emotions, and experiences in a genuine and healthy manner. Often, we ourselves are disconnected from our deep-seated fears, emotions, and thoughts. Consequently, when children express their emotions or articulate themselves, we feel at a loss. We become uncomfortable with their emotional outbursts and instead of possessing the emotional capacity to listen, we react defensively, labelling them as dramatic, difficult, or volatile.

Our early childhood experiences form an invisible patina of emotional experiences, influencing whether we feel connected, competent, and effective as parents. Our distortions of our own childhood and our perceptions of our parents create scripts within our minds that shape our parenting styles. We are conditioned to 'rescue' our parents rather than expect them to address their problems responsibly as healthy adults. Moreover, if a parent is overly strict, difficult, or struggling with compulsive behaviour or addiction, we are often discouraged from discussing our own challenges because of their behaviour. We are labelled as selfish and judged unfavourably if we do not admire a parent who may not have treated us well or who compared us unfavourably to others, all under the guise of motivation.

This idolisation of parents and reluctance to acknowledge how their actions made us feel depleted or fundamentally flawed often leads to unhealthy parenting patterns. When one feels flawed but refuses to acknowledge it, they inevitably pass it on to their children by incessantly criticising them, disapproving of them, or questioning every decision they make. Thus, parents who felt flawed as children unwittingly and unknowingly perpetuate feelings of inadequacy in their own children.

Alice Miller, in her book *The Drama of the Gifted Child*, eloquently emphasises this phenomenon, stating, 'When I used the word "gifted" in the title, I had in mind neither children who receive high grades in school nor children talented in a special way. I simply meant all of us who have survived . . . childhood thanks to an ability to adapt even to unspeakable cruelty by becoming numb . . . Without this "gift" offered us by nature, we would not have survived.'

At this moment, you have a choice to connect with your adolescent in a manner that prevents intergenerational trauma from further permeating their inner landscape. The cycle ends here. So, congratulations on being prepared and motivated to courageously halt this cycle of emotional numbing, disconnection, and volatility in your parenting approach.

Take this quiz below to kick-start your journey as a healthy parent who is ready to acknowledge their journey and become aware of what criticisms and hurts are buried deep within their mind. Remember, writing is cathartic. It releases suppressed hurts and pains. Furthermore, it gives you valuable insight into any issues that you may need to process with the help of a professional and licensed family counsellor or psychotherapist.

Did you ever get criticised as an adolescent?

Did you feel ashamed as an adolescent?

Did you have any family secrets that you were told not to share?

Did you ever get physically abused?

Did you ever get sexually abused?

Did you ever get emotionally abused?

Did you ever have an option to seek help for any trauma that you faced?

Did you find your parents controlling?

Did you feel scared of one/both of your parents?

Did you feel free to pursue your own dreams as an adolescent?

Answer these questions with honesty to connect the dots and see if your childhood holds the key to some of the current problems that you face today as a parent.

Now, let's explore your current mindset:

Do you feel that your adolescent child lacks a sense of responsibility?

Do you believe it's your moral obligation to monitor your teenager's behaviour?

Do you find yourself constantly feeling the need to check on your child for various reasons?

Do you frequently discuss with your child the importance of monitoring their diet?

Do you often talk to your child about their weight?

Do you frequently find yourself reminding them to be more active, sleep less, eat less, study more, etc.?

Do you feel the need to monitor your child's phone etiquette or the time they spend on their phone?

Do you frequently become irritated with your teenager?

Do you experience guilt after losing your temper with your teenager?

Do you sometimes find it difficult to maintain assertive yet respectful communication with them?

If you answered yes to two or more of these questions, are you willing to acknowledge the possibility that you are passing on the feelings of being flawed onto your adolescent. No one likes feeling defective about anything, whether big or small. No one appreciates being corrected, even when told 'I am telling you for your own good.' The fact remains that when we are corrected for something, we feel flawed. This undermines our floundering self-esteem and induces anxiety, even when we do understand why. One of the reasons that these days we hear of a majority of middle school and high school students struggling with mental health issues like eating disorders, insomnia, anxiety, panic etc., is that they feel flawed.

It is time that we accept that teenagers who become emotionally numb or come across as difficult are often struggling with self-worth issues. The reasons for this erosion of their self-worth often lie in our own homes and in our own parenting and our parental expectations. Parents often live vicariously through their children and expect them to fulfil their own unfulfilled aspirations.

Famous American child artist Jennette McCurdy wrote in her book, *I am Glad My Mom Died,* 'Yes, it's nice to make

Mom feel good, but it's also nice to feel good at something . . . Even if that thing is very stressful. Sometimes it is nice to feel good at something.'

Instead of confronting the possibility that, in the name of love, our parents goofed up their approach on healthy parenting, many of us as children, chose to shoulder the blame ourselves or internalise a flawed and dangerous belief system of 'I am not good enough.' This was not our fault. As young children entirely dependent on parents for survival, it was easier to accept our own incompetence or defectiveness than to question the sanity of their parenting or their ability to love unconditionally. No wonder, then, that intergenerational trauma persists across generations until a courageous adult emerges, capable of delving fearlessly into their own childhood and consciously nurture their inner world through self-awareness, clearing the debris of collected hurts from their psyche. Once an adult successfully releases themselves from toxic childhoods entanglements, they are ready to create a change within themselves and in their own approach to parenting. They can then embark on a journey of healthy parenting, recognising children as distinct individuals who bring the gift of parenthood.

As Kahlil Gibran said:

> Your children are not your children.
> They are sons and daughters of Life's longing for itself.
> They come through you but not from you.
> And though they are with you, yet they belong not to you.

So, to kickstart this journey as a healthy parent, review these key concepts over the next six weeks. If necessary, print out this checklist and organise it in a folder, dating each entry for the next 40 days to keep track of your progress. Remember, honesty is key. This list is for your eyes only, designed to facilitate your understanding as a parent. It's not a judgement or a preaching, but a simple compilation of helpful psychological concepts to alleviate concerns about parenting. Each of these twenty-five points is supported by ample scientific research, presented in simple language. A list of some relevant studies is included in a subsection at the end of this book, should you wish to explore further. Remember: Regular, daily practice is what will ultimately yield results.

Go through this checklist. Tick the ones you already practice. Circle the ones you wish to adopt. Mark with a star those you deem unnecessary. This is for your understanding of your thought processes and beliefs. The ticks portray healthy choices you are already making. The circles show avenues for growth and healthy choices. The stars are your areas of resistances and show you, quite clearly, what real hard work lies ahead for you in terms of explorations and change of mindset.

1. I am willing to accept that my attachment style with my parents impacts how I parent my child.
2. My child is not my foot soldier to fulfil my own desires.
3. My child is different from me, and that is okay.
4. Just because I think my child is more privileged than me, doesn't give me the right to remind them of this on a daily basis.
5. I am not a Shylock, demanding my pound of flesh from my child, simply because I do so much for them.
6. I can choose to trust God and believe that His plan

for my child is better than any that I can make for my child.

7. I am willing to speak to my child with respect and in a dignified manner.
8. I do not let my irritation or their conduct be an excuse to snap at them.
9. Every child deserves love, respect, and acceptance without any conditions of 'good' behaviour or 'good' emotions.
10. I am ready to let them think independently even when I don't agree with them.
11. I will not control, coerce, and threaten to make them do what I think is correct.
12. I am willing to seek outside help from a trained professional to ease our relationship.
13. I am willing to actively listen to them.
14. I am willing to refrain from blaming them, scolding them, or worse.
15. I choose to communicate in an assertive but respectful tone.
16. I cannot justify my emotional dysregulation by telling them that they made me do it.
17. I need to listen more than tell them what to do.
18. I am ready to role model behaviours and values that I expect from them.
19. I demonstrate my unconditional positive regard for them on a regular basis.
20. My own behaviours, thoughts, and beliefs are in alignment.

21. I am ready to refrain from mudslinging, verbally accusing, or fighting in front of them.
22. I consciously choose to be emotionally available to my child.
23. I am willing to explore the possibility that some of my behaviours are toxic for my child.
24. Approval from parents is important for every adolescent's well-being.
25. I am ready to love my child unconditionally.

One of the primary reasons why we feel overwhelmed, overloaded, or incompetent as parents is because we consistently adopt an external frame of reference. We believe we know what is best for our children and what they ought to think about specific situations. We fail to encourage them to operate from an internal frame of reference, nor do we show them how to do so. To be fair, this oversight often stems from our lack of education on these concepts and their significance in nurturing healthy relationships.

Upon grasping these concepts, we become more willing to employ them in our daily conduct. It's important to remember at this juncture that these mindsets evolve into habits through mindful choice. We need to incorporate this style of thinking as an integral part of our mental and emotional lifestyle. Only then will it manifest as an emotional ability resource, enhancing the quality of the parent-child relationship.

Many of us readily embrace a lifestyle focused on healthy choices concerning our physical well-being. This is because we are aware that consistent healthy choices regarding food, exercise, and sleep are essential for good health. We understand that there's no quick fix formula and are therefore prepared to invest the necessary effort into embracing a healthy lifestyle.

Now, the million-dollar question arises: Are you willing to apply the same approach to your parenting goals? Are you willing to explore healthier patterns of regular behaviour and invest time, effort, and energy into overcoming maladaptive thoughts and faulty beliefs that may hinder effective parenting? If your answer is a resounding yes, then read on.

2

Enhancing Adolescent Well-Being

'Don't worry that children never listen to you; worry that they are always watching you.'

—Robert Fulghum

When parents consider or discuss the well-being of their adolescents, what they effectively mean is the experience of good health, joy, and feeling satisfied with what one has in the current moment.

The popular concept of emotional well-being includes being focused but relaxed, calm, courteous, in good mental health, enjoying life to the fullest, feeling as though one has a purpose or meaning, and being able to cope with stress. Young people who are in good emotional health are better able to handle the difficulties of adolescence and make the transition to adulthood more smoothly. In fact, overall well-being in adolescence is linked to resilience, strength of character, emotional intelligence, good social skills, and effective coping mechanisms.

Confusion and Anxiety in Adolescents

Adolescents require a significant amount of empathy and understanding from their parents. Although they may not always express it directly, the reality is that many of their thoughts carry heavy burdens. They often harbour doubts about themselves across various aspects of their lives, even if they present a façade face of confidence. They go through a variety of challenges on a daily basis—their social aspirations, friendship and relationship issues, leadership development, balancing sports and extracurricular activities, raging hormones, parental aspirations for them, coping with distractions while trying to ace their grades, fear of not getting through a good college in the face of stiff competition, confusion about what to study, career choices, their looks, etc., the list is endless.

In any given week, an average teenager may feel helpless, hopeless, or unlovable—sometimes experiencing a mix of all three to varying degrees—due to various reasons. Their thoughts often skew towards panic, stress, anxiety, maladaptive coping behaviours, dysregulation, indicating chronic distress. These symptoms typically point to one specific truth: The teenager is struggling, period.

When unable to cope or manage, teenagers often find their minds in a state of confusion, leading them to implode without considering the consequences. At this point, what they need is ample support, compassion, kindness, and instinctive humanism from their parents. Any alternative approach typically proves counterproductive in the long run.

Name: Nitin Agarwal
Gender: Male (he/him/his)
Age: 17
Family type: Joint

While I was entering the puberty phase, with the numerous physical changes, I also had the urge to try new things. This led to me trying alcohol for the first time. The problem

> arose when it started to become a regular occurrence. Even though I was quite open with my parents, I felt like I was disrespecting their upbringing but was compelled to fit in with the social group. I felt like it was normal as all my friends were doing it, and I thought I could deal with it myself. Despite having left the habit of drinking, I still felt the weight of disobeying my parents. However, I failed to communicate this to them. With regret for my actions, the only solution I saw was to handle it myself. I reasoned to myself that they were also once my age, or that they would understand what I was going through as they would have had similar experiences. My conservative family worsened the situation. Every time I saw them, I would go on a guilt trip and force myself to keep it to myself, knowing I would let my parents down by confessing my mistakes. I wish I had the ability to make my parents understand the situation, but every time I thought of telling them, I would envision them being embarrassed of me and disappointed in my upbringing.

This is a case in point on how teenagers are concerned about being viewed as 'good' by their family members, especially parents. They want to be validated for who they are. They sense our disapproval, even when we do not voice it. No wonder they frequently are plagued by guilt.

To avoid such communication gaps, it is imperative that you learn to effectively communicate your unconditional love and validation to them. Further, a dialogue about what is appropriate and what is not is usually helpful in diffusing anxiety and clearing confusion.

When they act up, understand that it is a cry for connection. Maintaining an objective viewpoint towards their behaviours helps you, the parent, remain calm and in charge. If you get ruffled, it can lead to emotional dysregulation, further intensifying conflicts with them. Remember, your problem-solving approach rather than getting sucked into emotional turbulence is the need of the hour. As you explore your own blueprint of parenting—which was formed even before you were aware, shaped by your own early childhood experiences—you will understand why your thoughts get hijacked by the brain's amygdala, the seat of emotional outbursts. Usually, we feel triggered in situations with people we love due to unconscious emotional grinding and upheaval.

Your emotional intelligence as a parent is reflected in how you handle the difficult situations with your bundle of supercharged hormonal reflexes, aka your adolescent. The situation can be trying, taxing, or downright nerve-wrecking. But remember, you can choose to remain anchored in healthy parenting and demonstrate your emotional abilities. The choices remain in your hands, provided you are mindful of your own inner triggers, strengths, weaknesses, and limitations.

Parents need to stop making it personal. Instead, they need to take charge of the situation and learn newer ways to connect with their teenagers, which are effective as well as facilitative of mutual emotional well-being. They simply need to upskill their own parenting rather than get enmeshed in a war of words, or worse, indifference with their children.

It is helpful to view the challenges and distance in communication as a gap in the skills of parenting. They have not learnt how to manage the chronic distress in how they relate to their parents. By the time they are adolescents, most have given up trying to connect.

The reason is simple. They tend to have seen a lot of incongruences while growing up. Their parents tell them to be loving and kind to others, yet they see their parents screaming at each other over issues without the slightest hesitation. They are told to not raise their voices if they are unhappy with something, but they consistently face yelling whenever they are lazy or make minor mistakes. They are instructed to not watch TV before bedtime, but their parents seem to be glued to the latest on their gadgets.

This incongruence displayed time and again in behaviours that scream quite unequivocally 'do as I say, not as I do,' creates confusion in young minds. Patterns of incongruence lay the blueprint for many adolescent faulty behaviours earmarked by self-sabotage, dysregulation, or self-harm.

Parents often engage in these behaviours unconsciously, without realising the damage they can cause in the long run. While children do not react to them immediately, the groundwork is laid early on, just waiting for the right moment to lead to difficult behaviour in adolescence.

Adolescents, charged up with the upsurge in their developmental hormones as well as at the psychological development stage, are geared to try and change this control dynamics, believing that whoever is in charge need not be responsible for their actions and unhealthy thinking, even if they do not act out or voice it.

The lack of support that adolescents often complain about, which baffles parents, is usually because of unmet childhood needs for emotional connection, sometimes not just in the current adolescent but also in one or both parents, who—in spite of being adults now—are still stuck in an unresolved earlier psychosocial stage, for which therapy is recommended.

In cases of emotional unavailability, children develop an unsatiated hunger for connection and an internal alarm system. If left unaddressed, this can lead to breakdowns in communication between parents and adolescents, as the presence of each triggers strong reactions rather than responses.

Understanding the Foundations of Family Dynamics and Adolescent Behaviour

A family system tends to be very set in its ways and usually resists change, primarily due to the fact that dysfunctions tend to be woven into the ways people give weightage to the opinions of various family members. For example, there are unspoken rules about who can express an opinion regarding what is the right way to behave, act, or spend. While most parents tend to feel that children do not listen to them anymore and do exactly as they please, that is often just part of a larger picture. Children do not learn indifference, defiance, and emotional unavailability from the environment; they learn it before they even realise what they have subconsciously picked up. Their later interactions with peers are usually just trigger patterns that may have been dormant until that time. Usually, adolescence is the time when that tends to happen. Not taking responsibility for the simple truth that most of the challenging behaviours that trouble you in your adolescent have been mirrored by someone in the family is like the ostrich burying its head.

Let's honestly accept that many of the child's learnt behaviours have been picked up from home and family members, and that the influence of one's family of origin is the deepest. Once we acknowledge this simple fact, we become ready to clear the cobwebs from our own behaviours rather than focusing on fixing the child. A lot of misbehaviours and fractured communication from adolescents are just symptoms of deep-rooted patterns and problems in the family system.

Educators have known for decades that children pick up from the home environment before elsewhere. Their propensity to pick up maladaptive coping strategies like distracted behaviour, poor performance, violence, bullying, lack of focus, fighting, and victim mentality is developed from their own vulnerability to stressors and the lack of sufficient protective factors like harmony, warmth, and unconditional love in their lives.

Let's be honest. The first social microsome that a child is exposed to is their own family. The dynamics between their parents and how they relate to each other go a long way in shaping up healthy patterns, gender roles, and personal responsibilities. Often, key concepts related to self-esteem, respect, motivation, adaptive behaviours, teamwork, and communication are unspoken patterns that a child picks up while growing up.

The development theory of German-American psychoanalyst Erik Erikson presents a stage-by-stage progression of psychological development. It suggests that every human needs to fulfil specific tasks associated with each age group in order to progress functionally to the next stage of psychological development.

This theory highlights the psychological crisis faced by teenagers as 'Identity vs Role Confusion'. During this stage, teenagers navigate their challenges by exploring various choices, testing the waters, and eventually integrating them into a cohesive identity. Successfully completing this stage gives them a healthy, confident sense of self. Parental support plays a crucial role during this stage, providing teenagers with grounding and confidence to make decisions in areas such as academic pursuits, career choices, and primary romantic relationships.

Parents often fail to see the danger of constantly helicoptering and get caught in a riptide of control when parenting adolescents, as their own fears and instincts to protect the 'child' are often what kill communication between parents and their adolescents. As we know, during a riptide it is crucial to be able to think clearly and move with the current to safely navigate a dangerous situation. Yelling or swimming harder against it—i.e., fighting to prove your point of view—is counterproductive. When someone yells at us or when we are yelling, we operate from our brainstem that is hardwired to help us survive, not for reasoning or logic. The brain cortex helps be reasonable; so, for our cortex to be active, we first need to calm down. This satiates our survival instinct lodged in our brainstem as when the yelling ceases, the perceived threat disappears. Then our neural connections move on beyond the brainstem to the front part of the brain, i.e., the cortex.

Clearing our own head and being on the problem-solving mode rather than letting our fears about the situation control our behaviour, helps in that moment of panic or difficulty.

Parenting Styles

Research and theory on human development as well as the majority of cultural belief systems have long been predicated on the tenet that parents exert a direct and strong impact on their children through the process of social interaction. The act of parenting, also known as child upbringing, supports and encourages a child's physical, emotional, social, spiritual, and intellectual growth from infancy to adulthood. Parenting encompasses all aspects of raising a child, not only those related to a biological bond.

'Parenting style' is a psychological construct that represents the common methods parents employ to raise their children. The temperaments of the parent and the child have an impact on the parenting style, which is heavily influenced by one's own parents and culture.

The notion of parenting style is based on Baumrind's 1971 scientific paper's description of the three distinct parenting philosophies—authoritative, authoritarian, and permissive (1971). Later studies added a fourth style—neglectful to this list. Not every parent neatly fits into one of these four categories, but by and large, these broad categories describe the approaches of many.

Authoritative parents adopt the strategy that is generally regarded as the best one. These parents are more flexible and pragmatic. Self-control, autonomy, and internal motivation are more highly developed in children of authoritative parents. Children like boundaries, even if they do not show it, as it gives them a sense of safety. Healthy boundaries are essential to experience psychological safety. A child who grows up with this healthy parenting style manages to resolve the psychosocial task of this age range successfully. The result is an emotionally strong young adult who has successfully navigated the perilous waters of adolescence and emerged with a solid sense of identity anchored in self-worth.

Authoritarian parents keep a tight grip on their children. These children may experience social difficulties and may be more prone to be controlling, rigid, difficult, or authoritarian as adults. Although such parents may show their children care and warmth, permissive parents may not set many boundaries, as they might prioritise their child's friendships before their parent.

According to research, children of permissive parents may be more creative and feel more entitled, and they may also value 'taking' more than 'giving' in relationships. Uninvolved or disengaged parents, usually referred to as negligent parents, play a restricted role in parenting. They might not engage their children in discussion, play, or other activities for as long as other parents do, and they might not bother establishing house rules. Some children of negligent parents may struggle with self-control and adherence to norms outside of the home. Many of them tend to experience conflicts, brawls, or power struggles with authority figures. They may also become prone to self-sabotage, heightened thrill-seeking, unsafe sexual experimentation, and exhibit ancillary addictive behaviours. In extreme cases, juvenile delinquency also becomes a reality. Frankly, navigating adolescence is often challenging for them, setting the stage for numerous life challenges in adulthood and enduring struggles thereafter.

Adolescence is a crucial developmental stage during which parents and children must reevaluate their interactions (Laursen and Collins 2009). The degree to which teenagers accept their parents' attempts to socialise them is influenced by parenting styles, as proposed by Darling and Steinberg's (1993) integrative model. Adolescents are not only passive social beings when parents raise them in particular ways; rather, they actively participate in forming the parent-adolescent bond and interpreting parenting behaviour in ways that affect their own outcomes. Adolescents' perspectives on behavioural autonomy and the legitimacy of parental authority are particularly crucial to this psychological process (Darling et al. 2007).

Different parenting practices are associated with individual variances in adolescents' views on their autonomy. Authoritative parenting has been identified as the most advantageous for supporting the healthy, normal development of autonomy in children (Baumrind, 1991). On the other hand, indulgent and negligent parents fail to provide enough guidance and supervision, whereas authoritarian parents do. Teenagers with non-authoritative parents are more likely to have unfulfilled desires for behavioural autonomy (Bush and Peterson 2013).

In conclusion, a rich depth of emotional presence plays a vital role in healthy parent-child relationships. Fortunately, a healthy parenting style has a positive correlation with the overall well-being of adolescents. As the warmest and most consistent of the four parenting approaches, authoritative parenting supports teenagers' psychological growth. Additionally, it fosters good relationships and goal setting in life. Teenagers who perceive their parents as bossy, controlling, and authoritarian tend to experience more confusion in life and lower autonomy. Those with completely uninvolved parents, or those who view their parents as overly permissive, exhibit apathy towards goal setting and had experience lower personal development.

So, without much ado, reflect on these questions:

1. Can your child share their failures without you without the risk of receiving disapproval from you?
2. Can your child give you feedback on how they feel disappointed about something in you?
3. Do you accept the possibility that you may not have been a healthy parent?
4. Are you willing to work on becoming a healthier parent?
5. Would you like to acquire the skills of emotional intelligence and develop your own emotional ability resources?

Answer Key:

5 yes: You are absolutely ready and open to upskilling your parenting style.

4 yes: You are ready but have some reservations to embark on this journey of healthy parenting.

3 or below: I recommend seeing a licensed family therapist or psychotherapist to help you explore your own unmet childhood needs and issues that are impacting your skills as a parent.

If both the parents are overly strict, it tends to have a negative impact on adolescents' behaviour because they both demonstrate overly demanding, unreliable, and unbalanced attitudes toward their children.

Research has shown that adolescent well-being positively connects with authoritative parenting style and parent-adolescent connection. Parents will be happy to learn that healthy and positive parenting encourages life skills and emotional and psychological well-being. This parenting approach will result in happy, self-assured children who are emotionally strong and are equipped to handle life's problems at every stage.

3

Mapping Our Bonds: Recognising the Internal Dynamics of Connection

'Each of us weave a unique thread in the grand tapestry of the universe . . . That is what great parents do—they live on for centuries after their physical selves depart, through the thoughts and values that they have bequeathed to their children.'

—RamG Vallath

The internal dynamics of our relationships or connections are deemed to be very complicated and complex. People often believe that these dynamics depend on factors such as who the other person is, the nature of the relationship, the intensity of interactions, or how they behave towards us. However, the starting point of any connection is, to a large extent, determined by each individual's choices and capacity for connection.

Imagine our capacity for connection as a light socket to which one plugs into any electrical appliance. The type of plug points on the switchboard and sockets determine which plugs will fit in.

Similarly, the process of learning to connect or bond with others is actually quite simple. Our internal dynamics of connection trace back to how we, as infants, initially learnt to attach to others. Therefore, the answers to how we relate to others lie in our attachment styles.

Role of Attachment

Notable Cambridge psychologist Edward John Mostyn Bowlby pioneered an interesting concept called 'Attachment Theory' to explain how we learn to relate to each other in relationships. According to him, our perception as babies of the cadence of our relationship with our mother or any other primary caregiver impacts the richness and depth of the quality of all our future ones. Most of the difficulties we face in our interpersonal relationships, including parenting struggles, have their roots in our unmet childhood needs and how we internalise our early environment and are attached to our primary caregiver.

His research, spanning a lifetime, portrays why 'the infant and young child should experience a warm, intimate, and continuous relationship with his mother (or permanent mother substitute)'. However, for most young parents managing busy schedules and multiple priorities while raising young children is difficult. So, even if they enlist the help of multiple caregivers to initially cope, the extent of the unmet needs and its impact is rarely felt by parents, until the child hits adolescence.

Bowlby first suggested the idea of attachment in the 1980s to define the underlying connection between parent and child that is necessary for life and growth. Bowlby viewed attachment as a set of ordered behaviours—such as newborns' weeping, smiling, clinging, and closeness seeking—that are biologically based and promote infant-parent relationships and maximise survival. Infants display specific behaviours toward their caregivers. When a child is left alone by the mother, his response is indicative of the level of attachment. Further, Bowlby has scientifically demonstrated that an infant's early attachment patterns reflect in all its relationships, in adolescent parent-child relationships, and as adults in marriages and with their partners.

The theory demonstrates attachment patterns in times of stress, such as illness, strange surroundings, and being left alone, to feel safe and protected. When there is no stress, children exhibit less proximity-seeking behaviours and the attachment system encourages them to exhibit other adaptive behaviours that encourage environment exploration and mastery.

Attachment Styles

The type and level of care that parents give to their children vary, and as children age, their attachment experiences are consolidated into what are known as 'internal working models' of relationships.

Secure attachment is characterised by a perception of oneself as deserving of care and competent in mastering the environment, as well as a view of others as dependable and successful. Parental attunement and adequate responsiveness give rise to secure attachment. Children who are securely attached seek their caregivers quickly when they are in distress, but they also feel secure enough to explore their surroundings when things are going well.

In contrast, insecure anxious-avoidant attachment is linked to parental unavailability and harsh rejection. These children believe that they are unlovable and incapable of receiving love from their parents, and they perceive everyone else as harsh and uncaring towards them.

Anxious-ambivalent attachment is linked to parental inconsistency. These children believe they are incapable of maintaining the attention and care of others. However, if their attention can be attracted and maintained, they believe that others will be able to offer assistance.

Children who are anxious or ambivalent keep a close eye on their parents' presence and level of response, and they make more overt attempts to get their attention. Their focus on their parents' availability prevents them from properly exploring their surroundings. It is undeniable that parental attachment has a significant and positive influence on young to middle childhood development. Nearly every element of early childhood development, including neurocognitive growth and social-behavioural skills, has been demonstrated to be influenced by attachment.

Adolescence and Developmental Attachment Issues

Adolescence also poses a lifespan developmental attachment problem in general, which is to retain parental attachment while pursuing new social identities apart from the family and forming attachments to classmates and romantic interests. In reality, a strong attachment and emotional ties to parents promote a healthy transition to independence and maturity.

A strong base encourages exploration and the development of cognitive, social, and emotional competence. In short, evidence demonstrates that attachment security in adolescence has the same effect on development as it does in early childhood. Securely bonded adolescents are less likely to participate in excessive drinking, drug use, and risky sexual behaviour, according to studies of nonclinical samples.

Attachment security among females is associated with decreased incidence of teen pregnancy. From the ages of sixteen to eighteen, considerable improvements in social skills are predicted by attachment security in adolescence. Moreover, adolescents who are comfortable in their attachments handle the transition to high school better, have more fulfilling relationships, and fewer conflicts with their family and peers.

It is evident that secure attachment is crucial for successful teenage adjustment. While there will always be conflict in a parent-adolescent relationship, how they resolve those disputes and maintain their relationship is something that can be influenced with healthy parenting skills.

Teenagers who believe their parents are committed to the connection even in the midst of disagreement and who feel like they understand them do so with confidence as they head into early adulthood. Adolescents who have a strong connection with their parents do not shy away from conflict, exploration, or individuation, nor do they rush to become independent before they are ready.

Control and Parenting

Attachment theory emphasises the nature of the relationship between children and their caregivers (usually the parents). It has its roots in observations made by psychiatrists in World War II who noted the impaired physical, psychological, and social development of infants in hospitals and orphanages who were separated from their parents. After recognising that these children needed not just food but physical contact, the caregivers noticed vast improvements in their development. Clinical psychologists went on to propose theories of personality development called 'object relations' that highlighted these early mother-infant bonds.

Aborigines and other native tribals raise their children without using physical force or conditions like 'you better do this, or else . . .' In fact, they follow the laws of nature and teach children to be self -reliant. They are protective and yet, they are more interested in teaching them survival skills and letting them behave as independent beings from early years. They do not control their children and constantly tell them what is best for them. Instead, they rely on their innate parenting instincts and let the child blossom and develop their own life skills, which they are free to autonomously learn as they grow. This trust in a child's ability to manage themselves in the face of imminent danger builds a solid foundation of self-trust in the child that they will be able to cope with issues in life as and when they arise. By the time a native child is an adolescent, there are many ritualistic rites of passage to show the entire community's confidence in a child's ability to manage and survive on their own.

Parental control and forever preaching about what is good or bad for the child are rarely a part of the parental narrative or blueprint in these cultures. Sometimes, doing nothing sparks the creativity instinct in young children. Think back to the time when your adolescent was a five-year-old. Did they constantly jump from one class to another or a structured activity schedule? If that was the case, chances are that your child missed out on developing the skills of design thinking, divergent thinking, and thinking out of the box.

If your child is socially withdrawn, is it possible that, perhaps, it is because as a young child, they were constantly 'checked' for some mannerisms or for who they were? Children have their own personalities, traits, likes, dislikes, and preferences. Let them explore and gently listen to them and guide them. Ask them 'what is it that they get, when they do a specific thing?' As they learn to explore the 'why's' of their own thoughts without censorship, they develop autonomy, personal accountability, and self-control. Their internal locus of control develops, and they learn to think in a manner that is helpful for their growth and development.

Furthermore, as parents listen to them, they feel important and worthy. Over time, their confidence in themselves increases and they become responsible and skilled at adulting as they age. Healthy parenting involves a lot of openness and a willingness to listen to them and taking a cue from them. So, when there is imminent danger, they are more likely to listen to you. But, if you cry wolf and reprimand, reject, or panic at most of their actions, they are less likely to reach out to you when they face challenges as adolescents. When we do not approve of them on a regular basis, they grow up feeling defective or not good enough.

I have spoken to countless parents and one thing I know for a fact is that no parent wants their children to feel down in the dumps. So, this realisation that becoming skilled at parenting is an art is a step in the right direction. Acquiring skills is the right approach for any goal that has been set. So, congratulate yourself for finally crossing the biggest obstacle to healthy parenting—self-introspection.

The beauty of this healthy parenting journey is that you are in complete charge of the process as it is just about changing your thoughts, beliefs, and behaviours. As we know, the only thing that we can control is our thoughts, not others', and not our teenagers'. Healthy parenting involves setting an internal point of control in your interactions with your child. As you learn from your early parenting journey, you start shifting from a fixed mindset that thinks, '*Uff*, teenagers! They just don't listen,' to a mutually growth-oriented mindset.

The Art of War by Sun Tzu talks about spiritually centring yourself before you engage in any battle. So, as you gear up to communicate and bring your adolescent into your camp and end the daily battle of wills, understand that this process is akin to preparing for war—you need certain basic skills of emotional intelligence to create a win-win situation for all.

Remember, your calmness, flexibility, and unconditional love will do the trick. It is that simple. Try it, to believe it.

4

What Is Effective Parenting?

'Having a child is like getting a tattoo . . . on your face. You better be committed.'

—Elizabeth Gilbert

Effective parenting is defined as a set of parenting skills wherein parents can understand and fulfil the basic physical and psychological needs of the child. Here, parents have the emotional strength to remain stable while fulfilling their parenting role. They are resilient, and their expectations tend to be age-appropriate. They do not expect their children to be their caregivers or robots who are supposed to look after the parents' needs, superseding all other needs. They are in control of their thoughts and actions and do not blame children when things do not turn out as per their expectations. They encourage individual growth rather than stifling it. At the same time, they can strike the right balance and raise their children to be conscious of their social and familial roles, too. Thus, they are able to have a healthy relationship with their teenagers.

Charles Whitfield says, 'Healthy relationships are open, flexible, allow the fulfilment of one another's needs and rights, and support the mental, emotional, and spiritual growth of each person. While they are often intimate and close, their intensity has a flexible ebb and flow that respects each member's needs and allows each to grow as individuals.'

Thus, being committed to being an effective parent is important to do a good job of parenting. Being emotionally effective and healthy as a parent is being conscious of a teenager's emotions and consistently validating, comforting, and being present with them.

Not healthily engaging with teenagers can be disastrous. Problems such as drug abuse, overeating, poor classroom performance, indulging in unsafe sexual behaviours, and lack of motivation are just some issues that crop up as a result of ineffective parenting.

Teenagers who do not get to be children lose out on much of their sense of identity. Their current problems may lead them to the chambers of psychologists for stress, anxiety, academic performance, and behavioural issues, or to medical practitioners for medication for health-related issues, weight problems, addictions, mood disorders, and a host of other diseases. Often, their inability to cope effectively manifests as 'faulty' behaviours and earns them the sobriquet of 'troubled teens' by society, school authorities, and parents. Other teenagers who are struggling sometimes become like robots, displaying 'perfect' demeanours akin to wise old people in teenage bodies.

The good news is that with proper counselling and supportive psychotherapy, a lot of these psychological wounds can be healed. The bad news is that many teenagers go through years of difficulties in their personal lives and problems in relationships and work before they seek help.

Kairavi was one such teenager. These are some of the reflections from her that were her insight during her therapy work.

'My parents lived by the "what will people think?" philosophy. In social gatherings, we had the 'perfect family' image. But, once we came home, both of them underwent a complete personality change. From affable, gracious, smiling adults, they became two different people. My mother became like a bull in a China shop, constantly yelling. My father was completely silent, distant, and in a shell, physically, verbally, and emotionally. Yet, sometimes, I would hear them screaming at each other in the wee hours of the night. I would lie awake and pray hard for them to stop.

'In the daytime, when both were around, I always had a feeling of "preparing for battle" between them and how to diffuse the tension. I ensured that I gave them no trouble. I always kept busy. I studied hard in the hope that it would make my parents happy. I learnt early to try to bottle up any uncomfortable feelings I felt.

'I focused on academics throughout high school, with no distractions. I rarely confided in friends about what was happening at home. I felt I needed to be home and only felt safe whenever I was at home. I did not adjust well at my college campus and somehow scraped through the three years.

'I was burnt out by the time I completed college. My adult life felt boring, and work sucked. I was constantly yelling at work and got into scraps with my bosses. I always blamed them. I left two jobs in a huff. I felt no one understood me. When it got too much, I started partying hard, every night. I fought at the slightest pretext. I couldn't form and maintain relationships. By now, somehow, I kept away from my family, on an unconscious level. My weight spiralled out of control. I developed bulimia and alcohol-related issues.'

It was when her life completely went out of control that she sought therapy. Now, it has been three years. She has regained her confidence. She is in a steady relationship and has had a good job for more than a year. Her regular therapy and healthy lifestyle have taken care of weight, alcohol, and eating disorders.

The honest interaction in her therapy sessions helped her finally see herself, instead of being invisible. She realised that her weight gain was a way she was hiding her true self. As she identified her feelings and learnt to voice them, she started finding worth in just 'being'. She did not try to keep over-busy all the time. Sharing her story of what it truly felt like, growing up in her home, removed her sense of defectiveness and freed her from the invisible shame cycle that she had bound herself in. She let go of destructive patterns in relationships and slowly regained a sense of Self which was loving, compassionate, and human. As her psychological wounds healed, she was able to achieve a sense of balance in her personal and professional life and have healthy relationships with others.

As we can see from Kairavi's example, effective parenting is not optional. It is essential for the healthy development and growth of teenagers into healthy adults, without glitches.

The Most Effective Parenting Practices

Dr Gottman, who has spent a significant portion of the last 50 years understanding parent-child interactions, shows us a ray of light when it comes to healthy parenting. Based on in-depth interviews with parents, who provided information on their marriages, responses to their children's emotional experiences, and awareness of the importance of emotion in their lives, he has designed a foolproof parenting choice, which uses difficulties as opportunities for growth and strengthening the parent-child bond. I have found it particularly useful in helping bridge the gap between teenagers and parents.

Mentioned below are different parenting choices. Check what kind of a parent you are.

The Dismissing Parent	**The Disapproving Parent**	**The Liassez-Faire Parent**	**The Emotional Ability Coach**
Ignores or minimises a child's feelings	Many of the same traits as the dismissing parent but in a more detrimental way	Accepting the child's entire range of feelings without any restriction	Understands how feeling upset can bring closeness with the child
Neglects or avoids interacting with the child's emotions	The child's emotional display is evaluated and criticised	Provides little advice regarding behaviour	Understands and respects one's feelings
Desires a rapid reversal of the child's negative feelings	Emphasises adhering to ethical standards of conduct	Does not impose restrictions	Views the world of unpleasant emotions as a crucial parenting environment
Considers the child's feelings to be a demand to make things right	Believes that controlling unpleasant emotions is necessary	Believes that aside from letting bad feelings go, there is not much one can do about them	Avoids making fun of or minimising the child's uncomfor-table feelings

The Dismissing Parent	**The Disapproving Parent**	**The Liassez-Faire Parent**	**The Emotional Ability Coach**
Downplays the events that caused the emotion and minimises the child's feelings	Believes that emotions are weak and children need to be emotionally strong	Not a problem-solving tool for children	Omits guiding the child's appropriate emotions
Believes that most issues will resolve with time and avoids problem-solving with youngsters	Believes that feeling bad is pointless and and a waste of time	Believes that controlling unpleasant emotions is a simple matter of hydraulics—release the feeling, and the job is finished	Uses a child's emotional outbursts as an opportunity to listen, sympathise with comforting words and affection, help the child name the emotion they are experiencing, provide advice on controlling emotions, set boundaries and demonstrate

The Dismissing Parent	The Disapproving Parent	The Liassez-Faire Parent	The Emotional Ability Coach
			appropriate emotional expression, and teach problem-solving techniques

Effect of the parenting practice choice on children			
The Dismissing Parent	**The Disapproving Parent**	**The Liassez-Faire Parent**	**The Emotional Ability Coach**
They understand that their emotions are incorrect, improper, and unjustified. The way they feel could lead them to believe there is something fundament-lly wrong with them. They can struggle to control their emotions.	They understand that their emotions are incorrect, improper, and unjustified. The way they feel can lead them to believe there is something fundamentally wrong with them. They can struggle to control their emotions.	They do not develop emotional self-control. They struggle with focus, making friends, and getting along with other children.	They acquire the skills of problem-solving, mood control, and feeling confident in their intuition. They learn well, get along with others alone, and have a high sense of self-worth.

We need to show our emotional strength and agility by investing time and energy into imbibing the points as listed out for an 'emotion coach' parent by Dr Gottman. Our deepest love and empathy for our children are the foundation of the idea of 'emotion coaching'. While not all parents are naturally good at emotional coaching initially, however, they can surely develop the required skills.

This kind of parenting is an art that calls for regular practice. It is a lifestyle choice of emotional awareness towards scientifically embracing a healthy, functional parenting choice.

Ten Principles of Good Parenting

Good parenting is not a skill that a parent is born with. It is not even something that gets infused into a parent the moment a child is born to them. It is something that one needs to learn, akin to picking up the basics of grammar for good communication. While every child is born with a Language Acquisition Device (LAD) as pointed out by the researcher Noam Chomsky, individual flair in particular languages is honed with a specific set of skills. The same can be deemed true for parenting with aplomb.

It is true that the moment a child is born, instinctively, parents nurture their young ones across species. However, when challenges surface in parenting, understanding and practising these principles would be a good way to prepare for smooth sailing through the parenting waters.

1. **Demonstrate the Behaviour You Want to See:** Children learn by watching their parents. If you react instead of responding, they learn the same. If you want reasonable, soft-spoken teenagers, ask yourself if you have role-modelled that behaviour since they were born. If you

want them to adopt a particular behaviour, pause and ask yourself, 'What in my behaviour would be helpful to achieve this desired result?'

2. **Set an Intention to Remain Loving:** An intention to remain loving in all your interactions sets the tone for love being the primary mode of communication between parents and their children. Often, parents feel that rules need to be obeyed, come what may. But isn't that akin to demanding conformity at any cost? History stands as testimony to the fact that expecting absolute obedience is disastrous for everyone concerned. When views differ, be willing to express differences lovingly. Consistency in loving behaviour is one of the biggest hallmarks of good parenting.

   Giving in to unreasonable demands is not love. What is love is having an honest, frank conversation in a calm manner about why you feel a certain demand cannot be met, which is loving behaviour. Being willing to listen to them, without interrupting, is loving. Once they have said something, having a discussion and stating your point of view is loving. Remaining respectful, even when opinions differ or they press your buttons, without raising your voice, is a good starting point.

3. **There is No Such Thing as Too Much Love:** Flood them with loving behaviour. Look at them with warmth and approval, instead of a constant disapproving face. They are human, and human beings tend to make mistakes, knowingly and unknowingly. Parents often fear that being too loving may spoil the child. But that is not true. One can choose to remain loving, even while being firm.

4. **Reap the Benefits of Warm Touch:** A parent's warm, physical touch soothes the nerves and makes us feel loved. Hugs, gently nuzzling, stroking the hand or head, and approving nods and pats all fall under the category of non-sexual, intimate touch, which releases the hormone oxytocin in the nervous system, making humans feel "loved" and wanted. Touch is one of our basic five senses. It is also the earliest and one of the simplest ways to form bonds and forge healthy relationships. Babies who are frequently picked up and cooed to tend to be happier. A child who has been loved with gentle touches of approval, such as a pat on the back and many daily warm hugs, tends to grow up confident, secure, and loving. Even when teenagers say "ew" or wrinkle their noses, try to include one soft touch or a warm hug daily in your interaction with them. We can learn a lot about loving touch behaviour by watching documentaries on National Geographic, where parents in the animal kingdom hold onto their little ones with absolute love, a feeling that needs no words to express itself but is clearly visible. Charles Whitfield, in his book *Healing the Child Within*, suggests that 'It seems that to feel connected and cared for, we need to be hugged and touched . . . we need from four to twelve hugs a day as part of our health maintenance.'

5. **Show Authentic and Truthful Behaviours:** Remain truthful and authentic in most of your behaviours, especially in social occasions. Demonstrate uplifting, appreciative conversations in private and genuine warmth for people at large if you expect them to be warm in their interactions with you and others. There is no point in back-biting about others and then fawning at those same people

with fake smiles on social occasions. Children lose respect if their parents think one thing in private and display contrary behaviour in public. Chelsey Goodan, in her book *Underestimated: The Wisdom and Power of Teenage Girls*, states that 'teenage girls can see acutely through the show people put on to look good. It's why their insults are so cutting and accurate.' Teenagers are especially adept at seeing through facades and masks. If they express a point of view about others, let them vent. Listen patiently. Then, gently, outline your expectations regarding their derogatory comments. Do not expect perfection from them if your behaviour is not setting a good example. Remember, adults often engage in toxic comments daily without being mindful of it, for example, when you voice snide comments about others, have an unflattering opinion of an acquaintance's outfit, or gossip about the state of someone's marriage or affairs in a condescending manner.

6. **Be Involved, Interested, and Engaged:** Dr Gottman says, 'Being an involved parent takes time and is hard work, and it often means rethinking and rearranging your priorities. It frequently means sacrificing what you want to do for what your child needs to do. Be there mentally as well as physically.' It does not mean completing their responsibilities like projects or hiring tutors to oversee their homework. Homework helps children engage in learning and gets them interested and engaged with useful concepts that they can apply. 'Homework is a tool for teachers to know whether the child is learning or not,' says Steinberg on WebMD. 'If you do the homework, you're not letting the teacher know what the child is learning.'

7. **Be Flexible:** It is important to treat each child differently after understanding their strengths, vulnerabilities, and development. Keeping pace with your child's development as he or she grows up helps parents remain flexible. Keep age and its impact on the child's behaviour in mind. The 12-year-old who wants to talk to friends more than you is taking concrete steps towards forming their own circle of support and deeper social connections. The intellectual curiosity of your 13-year-old, when they confidently ask questions in the classroom, is also making them argumentative at home when they want to prove their point. It is important to stay consistent. Children get confused if parents expect something from them and then do the exact opposite in their own behaviour. If the child is expected to refrain from phone usage, other family members need to be mindful of their own usage too. If a parent is scrolling through Instagram and justifies it by saying they are working, so they can use their phone, the teenager is not likely to refrain from phone usage. Even if they do, this differential treatment is likely to breed resentment in them. Children usually treat others the way their parents treat them. They either copy them blindly, or they behave in absolutely opposite ways. Either way, their behaviour with others is significantly influenced by how they feel about how they have been treated. Gottman says, 'Your relationship with your child is the foundation for their relationships with others.'

8. **Set Fair Rules and Avoid Pushing Them Too Hard:** Pushing teenagers to do better rarely gets them motivated to improve. Even if they comply, sooner or later, most rebel and undermine your authority. There tend to be cracks in

your relationship with them if not handled with care. If the teenager is constantly demotivated, could it be due to lack of sleep, difficulty coping with different activities, lack of support from friends, or some other challenges they are facing? If this continues for more than two weeks, seeking help from a well-trained psychologist or counsellor may be helpful to accurately pinpoint the real issues and work towards resolving them in a healthy, age-appropriate manner. Explain the rules to them and the reasons for those rules. Share your fears, experiences, and the benefits that you see for them by following those rules. Remain willing to adapt if needed to reach a mutually comfortable point. If needed, seek help from a counsellor together to get an objective, healthy viewpoint and reach that sweet spot of mutual win-win.

9. **Refraining from Micromanaging Them:** Micromanaging teenagers inhibits their healthy growth and development of personal responsibility. Letting teenagers make choices is a way to foster personal responsibility. It demonstrates your faith in them. Further, it teaches them that there could be consequences to their actions if they are mindless. If they get bad grades due to being negligent in their studies before a term examination, they may be willing to get more serious about their preparations and spruce up their act for the annual examination. In time, they learn caution as well as personal accountability. Remember, learning to face consequences at 14 is better than being shielded at 14 and then facing harsher consequences later in life. This helps them achieve a balance and develop a sense of self-control and self-direction. Teenagers who are micromanaged tend to grow up to be confused adults. They tend to be indecisive, unsure how to take decisions for

themselves. They tend to have low self-esteem and a sense of worthlessness, where they constantly doubt themselves and their abilities. Sometimes, they grow up in exactly the other way. They misuse their freedom and indulge in excessive risky behaviours the moment they get a bit of freedom as they enter college. They have not developed a sense of boundaries, and their capacity to make healthy choices is often stunted, as they have never learnt how to make good choices while growing up. After all, practice makes us skilled at something, right?

10. **Understand Their Need for Independence:** Equating a child's need for independence with rebelliousness or disobedience is counterproductive. Teenagers are learning to navigate life and find a sense of balance between expectations, work, relationships, desires, and the need of the hour. In their journey to find their own notion of balance and feel in control of themselves, controlling them is usually counterproductive. No one likes being controlled by another human being. If explained properly, teenagers are actually quite reasonable. Often, parents overexplain to younger children and underexplain to adolescents. Take time out to have uninterrupted conversations about their growing independence. Meaningful conversations create safe spaces to talk about our deepest fears and desires. An open mindset builds strong bridges of connection. It encourages independence yet inhibits unnecessary risk-taking. With such support, teenagers learn to make good choices, instead of following their peers. A healthy discussion on changing values from one generation to another helps forge autonomy and a propensity for making healthy choices, with growing independence.

Neglecting to Prioritise the Child: A Common Oversight Among Parents

You work on various relationships—your friendships, marriage, and dating. But what about your relationship with your child? What truly matters is building a good relationship with your child and being in tune with them.

Parenting is the toughest and most rewarding job you can ever have. That's why parents often stick to what they know. However, not everything they try works perfectly all the time. That's why parents need to take time to reflect on their methods.

Most parents choose their parenting style unconsciously. Usually, their style either mirrors their parents' or takes a completely different path. Therefore, parents need to take a step back and figure out: 'Is this what I want to be my choice?' As parents, we're often in a rush and busy moving from one task to another, and we do not necessarily think mindfully about our parenting methods.

Something to Ponder Upon

Good parenting involves effective communication, leading to healthy interactions between parents and teenagers. As parents become increasingly skilled at good parenting, they grow more mindful of the impact their words and actions have on their children. They understand that teenagers are grappling with many uncomfortable emotions like guilt, shame, anger, sadness, and fear, which often sweep them into a flood of indecisiveness and self-doubt.

Forcing or controlling them severely is counterproductive. What proves productive is building one's emotional strength and fostering an open, flexible mindset. Conversations about expectations, and the willingness to tweak them to realistic levels, keeping in mind the child's age, environment, and social demographics, often yield the desired results of a deep connection as well as strengthening the bond with teenagers.

5

Building Rituals and Creating Spaces for Open Dialogue

'Raising children who are hopeful and who have the courage to be vulnerable means stepping back and letting them experience disappointment, deal with conflict, learn how to assert themselves, and have the opportunity to fail.'

—Brené Brown

Adolescence and adulthood are crucial stages of development that come with changes and challenges. One of the major challenges facing families of children, adolescents, and emerging adults is to help them develop better emotion regulation. Parents can use routines and rituals to create a sense of order and stability within the family, which can play an important role in developing better emotional regulation. Relationship routines and rituals can also contribute to a more stable environment, leading to better outcomes for individuals. Studies have shown that routines and rituals within a family can be predictors of better emotional regulation and outcomes for children and adolescents (Crespo, Davide, Costa, and Fletcher 2008; Fiese 2007; Leon and Jacobvitz 2003).

Raghav, at 15 years old, possessed an easy-going, affable demeanour, generally pleasant to be around. Rarely did he lose his composure when faced with adversity. Each evening, following dinner, he, alongside his parents, two siblings, and their dog, Goofy, assembled in the sitting room. Their discussions typically revolved around the day's triumphs and tribulations. From a young age, Raghav had learnt to articulate his emotions without becoming agitated. Even in disagreeable situations, he managed to voice his concerns with respect, mirroring the conduct of his parents. Raised in a household where shouting was taboo, he eagerly anticipated this daily half-hour routine from Monday to Friday.

Additionally, he had a passion for football. Often, he and his friend Karan would commute together to the field, alternating vehicles each day. However, Karan's chronic tardiness had become a source of frustration for Raghav over the years. Despite their deep-rooted friendship, Raghav refrained from addressing this issue with Karan, aware of Karan's tendency to react defensively when confronted. Raghav recognised that Karan's upbringing, marked by his father's short temper, had influenced his defensive demeanour.

Consequently, Raghav adopted a patient approach, allowing Karan time to cool off before broaching sensitive topics in a non-confrontational manner. Over time, this approach fostered trust between them, leading Karan to become less defensive in Raghav's presence. Therefore, when Karan once again delayed their plans, Raghav calmly expressed his disapproval. Although initially met with resistance and outbursts from Karan, Raghav's assertive yet composed response prompted Karan to reflect on his behaviour. Subsequently, Karan apologised via text, promising to correct his habitual tardiness. Raghav acknowledged the apology with a thumbs-up emoji. Fifteen minutes later, as they reunited downstairs, they exchanged a celebratory high-five before embarking on their journey, sharing a laugh over a trivial joke.

Research has focused on family relationships to identify risk and protective factors during adolescence. One of the most important tasks for families is to facilitate the development of self-regulation, specifically emotion regulation. This is accomplished through interactions between individual differences, such as temperament and emotional reactivity, and the psychological and social resources of the family. A proper fit between these factors can promote development and play a protective role, while a poor fit can expose individuals to risk factors (Compas et al. 1995; Compas and Reeslund 2009; Gross, Richards and John 2006; Martin 1987; Morris, Silk, Steinberg, Myers and Robinson 2007).

Relationship routines and rituals with teenagers by parents is a practice that has gained attention for its potential protective role in promoting positive outcomes in children, adolescents, and emerging adults. This practice may help develop self-regulation in adolescents and ultimately promote their ability to regulate themselves and their emotions. Routines and rituals are repetitive patterns of behaviour that, when performed by parents, help facilitate family life, instil family values, and strengthen family identity (Fiese 2006; Morris et al. 2007; Stocker, Richmond, Rhoades and Kiang 2007). These practices can vary greatly among different cultural and ethnic groups, and the importance of these practices can also differ among families within a certain cultural and ethnic group. After all, there are lots of priorities and commitments that every family emphasises. However, a lack of regular communication, more often than not, leads to disastrous consequences. Children thrive when there is clear communication and room to be themselves, even when they are unable to meet all their parents' expectations. Extreme rigidity, punitiveness, judgment, inadequacy, or constant criticism shrivel the healthy growth of teenagers.

Rituals play an essential role in shaping and transmitting shapes and values across generations (Fiese 1992; Selvini-Palazzoli, Boscolo, Cecchin, and Prata 1977). In all cultures, rituals have been used to create a sense of group identity and cohesion. Parents often engage in rituals for similar reasons, such as promoting family unity and organisation in meaningful ways (Wolin and Bennett 1984).

> Diya was 12 years old. She loved Diwali. She had been told that her name was inspired by the festival of lights. She had brought happiness into the lives of her family, so her mother had named her Diya. Every year for Diwali, they gathered together at her grandparents' ancestral home, which was one hour away from her home in Gurgaon. Her cousins, uncle, and aunt joined them, too. Even though they all lived on the outskirts of Delhi, meeting was a challenge due to conflicting work and school schedules.
>
> Every year, for two days, the entire family gathered and celebrated the festival. There was a lot of laughter and shared jokes. Her father and uncle often told them childhood stories of their Diwali celebrations. There was a sparkle in her dad's eyes as he recounted them. He seemed relaxed and at ease on those days. Usually, he seemed preoccupied at home. Diya rarely saw him except

on weekends. So, this annual ritual was special for her. It made her feel loved and glad to be a part of her family. Furthermore, with these anecdotes, she understood why her father thought in a certain way. To put it simply, these annual visits gave her insight into some of the rules in her home and helped her understand her parents' expectations a lot more. No wonder she was willing to listen to what her parents told her. Diya knew that she did not have to do anything by force.

This instilled confidence in Diya and she was able to focus on her studies and extracurricular activities at her own pace. Additionally, she seldom found herself in disagreements with her parents, unlike many of her peers. She considered herself fortunate and appreciative.

Research has shown that parental rituals are essential for an individual's psychological growth and adaptation. In a qualitative study conducted by Bossard and Boll (1950), they found that family rituals bring stability during stressful times and can influence family life positively.

However, some parenting rituals are counterproductive to the growth of teenagers. Sometimes, one parent, or both, may discuss family issues with their growing children and ask them not to discuss it with others as it is a 'family secret'. Occasionally, parents feel that it is okay to discuss their problems as that will help teenagers learn to solve problems. But would you send a teenager to fight a war on the borders without adequate training? So, when the parents talk to children, they only discuss their problems.

Often, such teenagers either act up, engage in risky behaviours, or become overly responsible when there is a lack of regular parental support or if parents are too caught up with their own issues. Good parenting involves creating an environment that lets children be their age. Teenagers are not meant to be proxy therapists. They do not possess the emotional maturity to listen to the problems that their parents face in their own adult relationships. If there is a lingering issue, it is recommended to seek help from a relationship expert or family therapist.

> Radhika was 14 years old. She was the class topper, and everyone in school thought that she was perfect. She was praised by the teachers for her good behaviour. Yet, Radhika internally cringed every single day. She had a 'family secret' that she did not want anyone to know. Her father was cold and distant and rarely saw him, even on weekends. He was always lost in his own world. Her mother was severely depressed and on medication. Sometimes, she did not get out of the bed for days. On other days, she went out by herself, dating other men and generally having a good time. She sometimes told Radhika about her night outs as also some of the issues she had with Radhika's father. She confided in her that she would have left her marriage, but she stayed because of Radhika.
>
> Radhika felt deeply ashamed and guilty about this 'family secret' and felt as though it was her fault. She coped by being very obedient to her mother and was hyper-focused on studies so that she could make her mother happy. She also rarely spoke to her father to show solidarity with her mother. She became fused with her mother's feelings and did not know how to feel until she looked at her mother's face every morning. She was unable to decide anything by herself. Radhika simply did what her mother expected her to do without a thought or protest. She had taken on the

role of a caretaker and started parenting her mother. She read everything in the library that she could find in the hope of fixing her parents' relationship.

In college, she took up psychology, and while going through the coursework and working on herself, she finally realised how toxic her teenage years had been even though everything seemed perfect on paper. She understood why none of her relationships had worked thus far, why she was constantly falling for men who needed to be reformed, and why her friends treated her shabbily. She realised that she had been emotionally numb since she was a teenager, and that is why she was unable to appreciate Life and was constantly feeling low. She also understood why none of her awards gave her any real joy, as she had learnt to live life on autopilot without learning self-love or assertiveness.

Therapy and intense self-work with the psychological tools that were now available to her, helped her recover and heal from the past. Accepting that she was worthy and not responsible for the troubles in her parents' lives was liberating. Regular mental self-care helped her rekindle joy in her heart, set healthy boundaries, and leave the caretaker mode behind. Radhika finally developed healthy relationships with everyone in her life.

Researchers are recognising that the meanings given to routines and rituals are key to determining their impact on individuals. Or has introduced the term 'ritual' and stressed the importance of understanding it from the perspective of the participants. 'Family time' not only refers to the time spent on routine and ritual practices but also the personal experience of investing time and emotion in them (Fiese 2006). Rituals are characterised by the symbolic meaning of the action for the participants and their commitment to continue that action into the future and pass it down to future generations. According to Fiese (2002) and Fiese & Tomcho (2001), the emotional and symbolic meanings of relationship rituals with teenagers communicate family identities and values. Doherty (1997) and Homer et al. (2007) highlight the importance of these rituals in conveying values and maintaining family relationships.

It is important to understand the significance and impact of family rituals when assessing their benefits for individuals and families. The meaning attached to these actions can moderate the relationship between the actions and outcomes, going beyond just the existence of routines and rituals. Various studies (Fiese & Kline, 1993; Fiese and Tomcho 2001; Fiese et al. 2002; Homer et al. 2007; Witz 2003; Marks 2004; Markson and Feese 2000) have suggested that if family rituals lose their symbolic meaning and become empty routines, they may not retain their benefits as meaningful rituals, such as promoting positive development in adolescents and young adults.

It is crucial for children to feel secure with their parents as it contributes to their emotional stability in the future. Positive parenting techniques play a significant role in establishing a strong connection with your child. Many parents assume that since it is their child, they don't need to consciously make an effort to connect with them. However, this is a misconception, and parents stand to benefit tremendously when they make a conscious effort to connect with their child and engage in effective parenting.

6

Parenting with Love

'Do you ever wonder how you can help your teens feel loved? Consider how they might tend to feel more appreciated through one specific love language.'

—Gary Chapman

Children need to be able to express themselves in a way that is of their choice. It may not necessarily be the way that parents express their emotions. One of the universal challenges in relationships is feeling loved the way we want. We can be vulnerable with our loved ones when they are willing to let us be as we are most comfortable and listen to us unconditionally. The concept of love languages has gained popularity over the last three decades due to its efficacy in improving relationships. The basic idea is especially fruitful when applied to parent-child relationships, especially with teenagers.

Teenagers comprehend their parents' love through the way they are treated. For them, love is an action word, not a verb. This implies that their sense of feeling loved is rooted in the actions they associate with being loved.

Before writing his 1992 book, *The Five Love Languages: : The Secret to Love That Lasts*, Dr Gary Chapman observed a pattern in the couples he had counselled. He found that the couples often misunderstood each other's needs. To simplify the expression and reception of love, Chapman came up with five different love languages. These are words of affirmation, quality time, receiving gifts, acts of service, and physical touch. Not everyone communicates love in the same way, and likewise, people receive love differently. To discover another person's love language, Chapman suggests observing how they express love to others, what they complain about most often, and what their significant other does.

He also suggests analysing what our teenagers most frequently request from us. Paying attention to their specific 'asks' can assist us in decoding their patterns. We can then understand which love language is best comprehended by them. Accordingly, if we reach out to them, we can deepen our connection and make them feel loved in a manner that appeals to them. The reason is simple. It is theorised that speaking to the other person in a language of love that they can understand can help strengthen the relationship and deepen bonds. Willingness to speak the other's love language shows interest, support, validation, and compassion for each other.

It has been observed that while parents kiss, hug, and physically offer comfort to young children under ten years of age frequently, they feel awkward doing the same with their teenagers. One reason for this could be that they feel their child is too grown up now. Another could be their perceived fear of rejection by teenagers. However, if a teenager's primary love language is physical touch, that child will feel unloved by parents if the parents do not offer enough hugs and kisses. Others prefer that their parents offer them words of encouragement. In Indian mythology, the famous warrior Maharana Pratap's mother is credited with offering words of encouragement that helped him develop into a fierce warrior when he grew up.

Here are some examples of love languages:

> Ankit is 14 years old. Every evening, he enjoys sitting with his father to discuss his day and hear about his father's day. His father is a banker. Ankit is fond of numbers and loves hearing about global trends, market movements, and financial matters. He extensively reads up on the topic so that he can engage in lively debates with his father. He prefers no one else to be around when they are talking and relishes the quality time they spend together. If his father is travelling, he misses their daily conversations. Gifts hold little importance for him; a new t-shirt generates as much excitement as any old one in his cupboard. His elder brother, who worked in an event company, frequently received opportunities and tickets to exciting city events. However, Ankit remained indifferent to the concert tickets arranged by his brother for him and his friends. The reason is that Ankit's preferred love language is quality time.
>
> Ishan is 11 years old and loves playing games. However, he dislikes doing chores, particularly watering the plants in their backyard, which he is supposed to do daily. Often neglecting this responsibility, his twin sister, Kyra, understands that Ishan may face trouble if he doesn't complete it. Consequently, she waters the plants every evening for him, creating a close bond between them. Ishan's love language is acts of service—when someone helps him by doing something for him, he feels cherished and loved.

Dr Gary Chapman's concept of love languages applies to both romantic and parental love. Understanding your child's love language is crucial for a healthy parent-child relationship. Here are the five love languages:

1. **Physical Touch:** Hugging and kissing are often considered ways to express love, but there are other ways as well. For instance, a father throwing his one-year-old son into the air, twirling his 7-year-old daughter until she bursts out laughing, or a mother reading a story to her 3-year-old on her lap. For children who understand this language of love, physical touch is a deeper form of love than simply saying 'I love you,' giving gifts, fixing a bike, or spending time together. Although they receive love in all forms, it is physical touch that has the clearest and loudest voice for them. Their love tank never fills up until they are physically nurtured in a warm embrace or a loving touch.

2. **Words of Affirmation:** Using words to express love can be incredibly powerful. Words that convey affection, praise, and encouragement are all ways of saying, 'I care about you.' Some useful words of affirmation that parents can use include:

    - I am proud of you.
    - Your hard work is praiseworthy.
    - You are enough.
    - We are blessed to have you.
    - We are confident that you are likely to succeed in achieving your goals.
    - I trust you.
    - I can see how hard you are working.
    - Thank you for doing this for me.

These words help to build a child's self-esteem and sense of security, and they are not easily forgotten. While all children benefit greatly from hearing positive words throughout their lives, teenagers whose primary love language is words of affirmation thrive when they get a regular dose of this love language.

3. **Quality Time:** Spending quality time with your child means giving your undivided attention. It's a way of conveying the message that they are important to you and that you love them. Quality time is not about the event itself, but about being present and engaged with your child during the activity. It's essential to go through the various stages of physical and emotional development while spending time with them. If quality time is your child's primary love language, it will help them feel secure and loved. Without adequate quality time and attention, children may develop fears that their parents do not genuinely care for them. So, make sure to spend quality time with your child regularly, giving them your full attention and care.

4. **Gifts:** Giving and receiving gifts are powerful ways of expressing love. The most meaningful gifts become symbols of love, and those who truly convey love become part of the language of love. Most children respond positively to gifts, but for some, receiving gifts is their primary love language. It may seem that all children are always begging for more, but the same can be said for adults. However, some individuals view receiving gifts as a way of expressing love. For them, receiving a gift is a strong signal of love and affection. They perceive the gift as an extension of the giver's love. So, it's important to

remember that for those individuals, receiving gifts is the loudest voice of love.

5. **Acts of Service:** Service is often viewed as the primary language of love by some people. If your child's primary love language is service, your acts of service are the most effective way to express your love for them. When your child requests you to fix their bike or a doll's dress, they are not only asking for a task to be done, but they are also seeking emotional love. If your child's primary love language is service, it doesn't necessarily mean that you must fulfil every request they make. It means that you need to comprehend that fulfilling their requests will help to fill their emotional tank.

Whatever the love language your child understands best, it needs to be expressed unconditionally. Unconditional love is the guiding light that shines in the darkness and helps parents know where they are and what they need to do to raise their children. Without that kind of love, parenting is a mess. Unconditional love can best be defined by showing what unconditional love *does*. It demonstrates the unwavering love of a child, irrespective of any factors. As parents, we love our children no matter how they look, the assets or liabilities they possess, or any disabilities they may have. We hold on to this love, no matter what we expect of them, and even when they behave badly. This does not imply that we approve of everything they do. It simply means that we communicate our love to them through our words and actions.

7

Managing Parental Irritability

'More of our kids are ruined by the behaviour of their parents than by the amount of the inheritance.'

—Warren Buffet

Anger is a natural response of the body to what it perceives as a threat. When a person feels angry, their body releases adrenaline, which makes their muscles tense up, increases their heart rate and blood pressure, and causes their face and hands to turn red. Different factors, such as one's nature, brain chemistry, or a disease can trigger anger in a person. Some common triggers for anger include a lack of patience, feeling unappreciated, worrying about problems, or reminders of past traumas. People who aren't taught ways to express and manage their anger as children are more likely to experience outbursts in adulthood.

According to a review by Thartori et al. (2019), the maternal innate tendency to react hyper-sensitively and aggressively when stimulated or stressed may lead to more punitive and maladaptive parenting styles, which can increase the risk of behaviour problems in a child. In this review, it was found that some parents who exhibit hypersensitive behaviours like yelling and sudden outbursts of anger might be modelling these behaviours on their children, which can lead to a negative spiral of hypersensitive parent-child interactions.

The teenage years are a critical time for any family as they face common challenges. Adolescents face extreme hormonal and emotional changes that are reflected in how they treat themselves and others around them. Teenagers feel misunderstood when they believe that no one understands their emotions. They often face their first significant constraint from their parents. During this stage of development, they may experience loneliness, anger, or confusion as they navigate important issues such as identity, peer relationships, sexual behaviour, and substance use. As a result, parents may feel frustrated or upset when their child doesn't adhere to rules and guidance. The methods of discipline that were once effective may now seem ineffective, leaving parents feeling helpless in raising their teenage children. Many parents live in constant fear of their adolescents making harmful decisions.

Relationships between parents and teenagers tend to be conflict-ridden due to issues such as choice of friends, ways of spending time, academic performance, substance problems, dating, relationships, and sexuality. Furthermore, there is a difference in opinion on the way they dress, general grooming, and use of make-up (Lachance, Burrus, and Scott 2012). Teenagers who seek identity and autonomy may eventually come into conflict with their parents. As they grow up and become more independent, responsible, and autonomous, it is important to provide them with gradual freedom. However, parents must remain vigilant and ensure that their children do not engage in risky and self-destructive behaviours.

Parents often feel angry and upset with their children because they fail to meet their expectations. Truly connecting with adolescents is where the parents fall short, which often leads to conflicts and dilemmas, leading to burst outs in the form of anger. Parents can get easily annoyed by certain behaviours of their teenagers. These behaviours include delaying tasks, repeated refusal to comply with rules, unwelcome displays of independence, and asking too many questions that may provoke objection. As a result, parents may become angry and resort to punitive measures to express their displeasure. However, it is important to maintain open communication with teens and avoid letting their emotions get in the way of productive conversations.

According to *When Anger Hurts Your Child*, authors Kim Paleg, Matthew McKay, and Patrick Fanning found that the following appears to be true: 1) Children of angry parents are more aggressive and less obedient and 2) Children of angry parents have less empathy and overall lower adaptive abilities. Moreover, anger and crime are closely related, as parental anger can have lasting effects on mental health, social exclusion, spousal abuse, and professional and financial failures later in life.

It is noted that the main problem with young people is that they imitate their parents' behaviour. Parents often believe that keeping their anger and ego helps them parent better. Instead, unbeknownst to them, it scares their children and makes them feel uneasy. Anger affects them forever, especially if it comes from a parent. When parents are angry or stressed, children may exhibit symptoms such as difficulty concentrating, trouble interacting with peers, anxiety, aggression, and sleep disturbance, all of which can impact their overall development. Studies have shown that escalating physical violence, such as hitting, can have lasting effects later in a child's life. Other studies have also shown that harsh parenting leads to negative outcomes for children. One study found that children who were spanked frequently were more likely to struggle in school, be diagnosed with mental illness, and exhibit antisocial behaviour.

Interactions between children and parents play a crucial role in the development of adolescent emotion regulation (Morris et al. 2007; Thompson 1994). For example, parenting styles such as a hostile upbringing (Jaffe et al. 2010), parental conflict (Fosco & Grych 2007), and parental negativity (Eisenberg et al. 1998) have all been associated with a higher prevalence of negative traits in children. Previous studies have suggested that the inability of parents, particularly mothers, to regulate their own emotions may contribute to this negative impact (Eisenberg et al. 2001; Thompson 1994). Thompson (1994) argued that when children are exposed to parental emotional repression for extended periods, they may emulate their parents' behaviour and develop similar emotional modelling strategies. Adolescents with high levels of anger may respond with self-shaming and self-blame to the risk of losing control (Cramus 1989). It is important to note that parental anger can hurt children. This can lead to indirect pathways such as shame, helplessness, and self-blame, which can be expressed by young adults (Kaplan and Liu 1999). Studies have shown that exposure to parental anger can cause embarrassment, self-loathing, and ultimately heightened self-blame in young adults (Butler et al. 2018).

A secure parent-child relationship helps children feel supported and emotionally safe, enabling them to express their feelings freely. This is a prerequisite for effective emotional regulation—an emotional environment in which children feel intimacy and warmth facilitates the expression of their feelings more comfortably. Furthermore, maternal emotional and cognitive regulation is associated with parents who are more likely to engage and respond. Recognising your child's emotional signals and responding in a supportive way are crucial.

In addition to warmth and support, positive parenting often includes clear rules and boundaries that help children know what to expect regarding emotional expression at home (authoritative parenting). This helps children express their emotions in a socially acceptable manner, for example, 'It's okay to get angry, but not to hit.'

Gottman, Katz, and Hooven suggested that parents who coach their children's emotions through problem-solving, emotion naming, and comforting the child encourage successful emotional regulation. This is in contrast to parents who ignore their children's emotions by belittling or punishing them for expressing themselves. Children and adolescents whose parents emotionally guide them are better able to manage their emotions than those who do not receive such guidance. In a study of adolescents, those who reported that their parents had taught them how to deal with anger and sadness were better equipped to manage their own emotions. These results are consistent with another study that found parental emotional coaching to be significantly and positively associated with children's emotional regulation and vagal tone. Additionally, other studies have shown that negative parenting practices, such as devaluing emotions, are associated with lower levels of emotional regulation.

It has also been proven that parental emotional support, positive influence, emotional coaching, and the use of shared strategies are associated with more effective emotional regulation in children. In contrast, psychological control, parental indulgence, expressed anger, and criticism are associated with emotional regulation difficulties in children.

Additionally, emotional regulation is one of the ways parenting influences children's adaptations, which can particularly affect emotionally reactive children. Moreover, adolescents reported being more positively affected when they were with their parents than when they were alone, and they also helped their parents regulate their emotions. It can be firmly established that parents highly influence emotional regulation in all adolescents.

8
Cognitive Behavioural Therapy to Improve Parent-Teen Communication

'The stronger person is not the one making the most noise but the one who can quietly direct the conversation toward defining and solving problems.'

—Aaron T. Beck

People are sociable creatures by nature. Social, emotional, and physical health rely on the relationships we have with others. Establishing and maintaining these relationships can provide a person with the strength to face life's challenges by enabling them to create a network of allies.

Interpersonal relationships refer to social connections between two or more individuals. These connections may include spouses, family members, best friends, acquaintances, coworkers, and various other people. Effective communication is believed to be the foundation of every interpersonal interaction. Maintaining strong and enduring connections depends on this. Without effective communication, problems will inevitably arise and relationships will suffer. Communication is crucial for preventing misinterpretations and establishing interpersonal ties. Diverse forms of communication need to be used to express and reciprocate sentiments in a healthy partnership. Nonverbal interactions such as facial expressions, hand motions, body language, and gestures are also important in conveying feelings. Interpersonal relationships are formed by people who share similar preferences, viewpoints, objectives, and interests, and compatibility is crucial in these relationships.

Interpersonal issues, defined as persistent difficulties in social relationships with other people (Davies-Osterkamp et al. 1996), are one element linked to the emergence and maintenance of psychological issues (Horowitz et al. 1993). A wide range of potential issues, such as being overly submissive or domineering, can cause interpersonal problems and disrupt a person's daily life. In a recent study evaluating the impact of interpersonal issues on group Cognitive Behavioural Therapy (CBT) outcomes for depression, it was discovered that difficulties with assertiveness and a propensity to ignore one's own needs were linked to worse outcomes, while difficulties with offering support to others or being honest about one's problems were linked to higher attrition (McEvoy, Burgess, and Nathan 2013).

People frequently seek counselling because of interpersonal issues. Often, people bring up issues where they're facing difficulty interacting with others in day-to-day settings, such as getting irritated by their partner's behaviour, finding it difficult to handle their child's behaviour, or acting aggressively towards others. Or they could be struggling with more entrenched patterns of communication in all their relationships, like concerns about not fitting in, frequently selecting violent partners, or not having their needs met.

CBT is a form of psychological treatment useful for a variety of issues, including depression, anxiety disorders, difficulties with alcohol and other drugs, marital issues, eating disorders, and serious mental illnesses. Numerous studies have found that CBT significantly enhances functioning and quality of life. It has been shown in numerous studies that CBT is equally successful as—or even more effective than—other types of psychological therapy or psychiatric drugs. The main goal of CBT is to evaluate and change problematic thought patterns and behavioural patterns. In order to change and improve communication styles, it is one of the most effective approaches to untangling ineffective communication strategies. This may necessitate addressing some of your beliefs in relationships, yourself, what makes you vulnerable, and how others who matter can understand you.

CBT is a useful method to understand complex situations and negative responses to them. It primarily focuses on three factors—thoughts, emotions, and behaviours, which are all closely linked to psychological issues. By breaking down difficult emotions into these three elements, it becomes evident where and how to intervene when a problem arises. If negative thinking leads to bad emotions and actions, re-examining these thoughts may be the best way to proceed. On the other hand, if a behavioural pattern is responsible for the issue, adopting a new and positive response to the situation could be helpful.

Some techniques that can help improve interpersonal relations are:

- Acknowledging and embracing the perceptions and expectations of each individual
- Investigating counterproductive causes, attitudes, and behaviours
- Deciding on alternative and appropriate tolerance ranges

- Recognising and implementing new behaviours based on mutual respect, shared values, empathy, trust, and tolerance
- A new 'emotional contract' articulates the changes each partner agrees to make and serves as the foundation for their future relationship

Freud, Jung, Adler, and Rank's psychoanalytic research has proven that unconscious motivation for behaviour exists. According to numerous clinical investigations into the causes of unconscious emotional conflicts, interpersonal interactions are crucial in the formation of personality. It has been discovered that parent-child relationships play a significant role in the formation of fundamental attitudes. Harry Stack Sullivan (1892–1949) emphasised the significance of interpersonal interactions by making perceptive and precise clinical observations. He paved the way for the current heavy emphasis on the environment and interpersonal relationships as psychological variables in many emotional illnesses by highlighting communication processes in interpersonal behaviour.

CBT helps teenagers change these incorrect cognitive patterns to improve their relationships with their parents and to foster positive feelings and behaviours instead of negative ones.

CBT interventions for teens include the following approaches:

1. **Cognitive Reconstruction:** In this practice, the therapist helps the patient identify the unfavourable thought patterns they frequently revert to, such as overgeneralising or always assuming the worst. Therapists can also

instruct parents on how to reframe their child's negative thought patterns positively. This involvement of parents in understanding their children and taking an interest in their lives can improve the parent-child relationship.

2. **Journalling:** The benefits of journaling are enormous. Many teenagers find that writing about their tension, worry, and anxiety helps them to distance themselves from these feelings and come back to the present. A diary also enables individuals to monitor how their daily writing is affected by their activities, hormonal fluctuations, food, and exercise.

3. **Social Roleplay:** Teenagers might utilise role-play to explore different situations that make them feel anxious or worried. Parents should treat teenagers as adults, soliciting their thoughts, presenting them with options, and encouraging them to find solutions to problems as they arise. Through role-play, teenagers can be empowered to speak up, defend themselves, and respect their boundaries, thus, becoming more certain and secure as a result.

4. **Gradual Exposure:** Teenagers can overcome their concerns or problems through gradual exposure. A family member can assist a teen in progressively exposing themselves to specific locations or activities that may trigger post-traumatic stress disorder (PTSD), anxiety, or depression, without endangering their mental health or safety.

5. **Mindfulness:** Through simple breathing exercises and other techniques, mindfulness helps people concentrate on the present moment. This practice reduces anxiety,

> boosts self-esteem, and sharpens focus. Parents should provide their children with space to explore their feelings, and, if necessary, ask for their assistance.

CBT assists patients in changing their behaviour through a variety of activities, much like other behavioural therapies. It helps people set healthier limits for their mental and physical health, over time, by reducing trauma and addiction triggers, altering negative thought patterns and changing harmful ones. CBT aids young adults in understanding their emotions, fostering emotional toughness and managing stress daily. Self-harm, substance abuse, and process addictions, such as those related to video games or social media, can all be decreased as a result.

9

LIFE TRANSITIONS: A GUIDE FOR TEENS

'In any given moment we have two options: to step forward into growth or to step back into safety.'
—Abraham Maslow

Life transitions refer to significant changes in a person's life that can include developmental milestones, personal and professional changes, and major life events that affect one's identity, relationships, and well-being. Examples of life transitions include marriage, parenthood, career changes, retirement, loss of a loved one, illness, and other life-changing experiences that can cause stress, uncertainty, and emotional upheaval. Coping with life transitions involves adapting to new roles, managing emotions, seeking support, and finding ways to maintain a sense of stability and meaning during the transition.

One of the most significant life transitions is the one from adolescence to adulthood. This transition can be both exciting and scary, as it often involves leaving the comfort and familiarity of home and entering a world that is full of new challenges and responsibilities. This involves making decisions about education, career, relationships, and more. It is a time when we begin to define who we are and what we want from life.

Divorce is a major life change that can be quite challenging to navigate. When a marriage comes to an end, it can feel as though a part of ourselves has died. We may experience emotions such as anger, sadness, or betrayal, and it can be tough for us to regain our balance in the world. However, divorce can also be a time of growth and self-discovery. It provides us with an opportunity to reevaluate our priorities and make changes that can lead to a more satisfying and fulfilling life.

Losing a loved one is another difficult life transition to cope with. It can leave us feeling lost and alone, struggling to find meaning in our lives. However, as we grieve, we may discover new strength and resilience that we didn't realise we had. We learn to appreciate the present moment and cherish the memories of our loved ones.

Life transitions are an inevitable part of life. They might be challenging, unpredictable, and difficult to navigate, but they also offer opportunities for growth and self-discovery. By accepting the changes that come our way learning to adapt to new situations, we can thrive and flourish. Whether we are transitioning from adolescence to adulthood, getting married, going through a divorce, or experiencing the death of a loved one, we can discover new ways to define ourselves and live our lives to the fullest.

Life transitions can be difficult to navigate due to several reasons. These may include the uncertainty of the future, the loss of familiarity and routine, the need to adjust to new environments and social dynamics, and the emotional stress of leaving behind people, places, or situations that we may have grown attached to. Transitions can also require significant effort and resources to adapt, cope, and overcome obstacles, which can lead to feelings of overwhelm, anxiety, and self-doubt. Moreover, certain life transitions such as ageing, illness, or loss can trigger deeper existential questions and emotional struggles, which can make the process of adaptation and acceptance even more challenging.

1. **Change Is Hard:** Life transitions usually involve a change in routine, lifestyle, or environment. Change can be hard for many people as it requires adjustment and adaptation.

2. **Uncertainty:** Life transitions can bring a sense of uncertainty about the future. This can be overwhelming and cause anxiety and stress.

3. **Loss:** Life transitions often involve leaving something behind. This loss can take the form of a relationship, job, or home. It can be difficult to move on from something that was once familiar and comforting.

4. **Fear:** The fear of the unknown can be a significant challenge during life transitions. Fear of failure, rejection, or not being able to handle new situations can be daunting.

5. **Identity crisis:** Life transitions can bring about an identity crisis. When transitioning from one phase of life to another, one's sense of self can be shaken, leaving them questioning who they are and what their purpose is.

6. **Loneliness:** Life transitions can be lonely, especially if you are leaving behind a social support system. It can be challenging to make new connections and build new relationships.

7. **Pressure:** There can be a lot of pressure during life transitions to make the right decisions and to do things 'the right way'. This pressure can be overwhelming and make it difficult to make choices that feel right for you.

8. **Resistance:** People may resist life transitions because they are comfortable with their current situation, even if it is not fulfilling or healthy. This resistance can make it challenging to move forward and embrace change.

There are numerous ways to categorise stages of life transitions, but one common framework is:

- Childhood: Infancy, early childhood, middle childhood
- Adolescence: Early adolescence, middle adolescence, late adolescence
- Adulthood: Early adulthood, middle adulthood, late adulthood
- Older adulthood: Young-old, old-old, oldest-old

These stages are typically characterised by physical, cognitive, and social changes and challenges, as well as shifting roles and expectations. However, it is important to note that each person's experience is unique and that they may not go through these stages at the same time or in the same way.

The teenage or adolescent years are defined by a variety of emotions and reactions on a daily basis as they transition from childhood to adulthood. This process is aggravated by the losses they experience. It is the responsibility of the adults in their lives to help them understand, absorb, and deal with these occurrences.

1. Adolescents go through various life transitions as they move from childhood to adulthood.
2. These transitions include physical changes such as puberty and growth spurts.
3. They also experience cognitive and emotional changes, such as increased reasoning abilities and understanding complex concepts.
4. Adolescents also experience social changes, such as the need for more independence and the development of peer relationships.
5. These transitions can be challenging and stressful, as adolescents struggle to adapt to new roles and responsibilities.
6. The support of family, friends, and other trusted adults can be crucial in helping adolescents navigate these transitions successfully.
7. Transitions during adolescence can also have long-term impacts on development and well-being, highlighting the importance of providing resources and support during this critical period.

Teens go through several life transitions, such as:

- Puberty and physical changes
- Increased independence and autonomy
- Developing a sense of identity and self-awareness
- Changes in relationships with family and peers
- Making decisions about their future, such as college or career choices

- Facing new challenges and responsibilities, such as driving or finding a job
- Experiencing the emotional ups and downs of adolescence, including mood swings and self-doubt
- Exploring romantic and sexual relationships
- Learning to manage their own time and prioritise responsibilities
- Coping with societal expectations and pressures, such as academic performance and social status

It is important for adults to have an understanding of the concerns that arise during teenage development and the grieving process, to avoid any unnecessary complications or overlooking warning signs. It is beneficial to reassure teenagers that the strong emotions they may feel in the moment will eventually pass with time.

Here are some tips to keep in mind:

1. Listen without passing judgement. Teenagers should be respected and understood since their need for independence makes them sensitive to adult judgement or criticism, which may prevent them from seeking comfort when needed.
2. Adults must be mindful of their grief and needs. Teenagers should not be assigned the role of confidant to adults. They must be able to rely on adults for support and safety.
3. Accept and expect a drop in academic performance. Parents should adjust their expectations to reflect a teenager's ability to cope with and function while grieving.

4. Respect the right to privacy. Adolescents require a haven as well as time to mourn their loss.
5. Recognise your teenager's ability to think abstractly. Their reasoning and debates will be guided by this cognitive process.
6. Accept the philosophical ideas they share as their way of making sense of the loss they are experiencing.
7. If possible, it would be helpful to provide context when discussing with teenagers so that their opinions and thoughts can be better understood.

Here are some coping skills that may help teenagers during life transitions:

1. **Communication:** Talking with trusted friends or family members about your thoughts and feelings can help reduce stress and anxiety.
2. **Exercise:** Regular physical activity, such as jogging or yoga, can help alleviate stress and improve mood.
3. **Mindfulness:** Practising mindfulness techniques like deep breathing, meditation, or visualisation can aid in stress management and promote relaxation.
4. **Self-care:** Engaging in activities you enjoy, such as reading, listening to music, or taking a relaxing bath, can help you take a break from stress.
5. **Seeking professional help:** If you find that stress and anxiety are affecting your daily life, it is important to seek help from a professional therapist or counsellor.

6. **Prepare whenever possible:** Try to prepare for your transition as much as possible. This could be as simple as creating a helpful mentality or laying out a strategy for the specifics of your transition.
7. **Have realistic expectations:** Frustration and stress can result from unfulfilled expectations. When a transition does not go as planned, it is important to set reasonable expectations that you will likely experience times of stress and overwhelm. It's also helpful to keep in mind that it's perfectly normal to feel stressed out during transitions.
8. **Establish a routine:** A routine can assist you in adjusting to a change. To help you feel more consistent, think about creating routines in the morning and at night. A daily walk, meditation, or intention-setting for the day, as well as regular sleep and wake times, can be beneficial additions to your routine.
9. **Check how you talk to yourself:** What are you saying to yourself in particular? Are these internal remarks assisting you in navigating this transition or making it more difficult? Recalling transitions (or other difficult situations) you have successfully handled in the past is one way to develop helpful self-talk. They could serve as a reminder that you can handle this as well.
10. **Set modest targets:** Set small, achievable goals that you can accomplish one at a time rather than attempting to resolve everything associated with your transition. Consider the following question: 'What is the one small thing I can do right now?' Contacting a broker about a new apartment, making an appointment with a doctor, or responding to a friend's text are all examples of this.

11. **Maintain contact:** During a transition, support from others is essential. Talking to a friend or family member can help you feel less alone.
12. **Show yourself compassion:** Change is challenging. The fact is that you will not always be able to successfully transition through life. Be kind and understanding to yourself during this time, even though these suggestions can help make transitions a little easier. If you have no idea how to proceed, ask yourself: 'What would I say to my best friend if they were in this situation to be supportive?' Then make the same declaration to yourself. Try this if you are unsure of what you would say: 'When navigating a life change, it is normal to feel overwhelmed or stressed. I am just going to try my best in this situation.'

Being prepared for life transitions enables teenagers to move towards healthy life choices. It enriches their overall experience of that phase, whether smooth, difficult, or both. Teenagers learn to move ahead with personal responsibility, accountability, growth, learning, and development. Examining core belief systems, working on faulty patterns, and changing behaviours empower them to make lemonade out of lemons. Building a deep connection with oneself fosters emotional well-being regardless of the overall climate of that phase.

10

Nurturing Autonomy and Emotional Health in Teenagers

'Children are apt to live up to what you believe of them.'
—Lady Bird Johnson

Is it a good idea if the teenager listens all the time? Absolutely not! But why so? Sometimes, some teenagers bend over backwards to remain in their parents' good books, regardless of their thought process. Worse, they imbibe the 'fawn' tendency that can lead to people-pleasing or becoming a fixer, taking a personal toll on their health, well-being, and mental health throughout their lives.

They learn that to navigate choppy waters and difficult circumstances:

- 'I must always please the other person even when I do not feel good because it makes them feel good.'
- 'I must be perfect or ideal so that no one gets upset or inconvenienced by my failures or mistakes.'
- 'It is okay to tolerate name-calling, screaming, gaslighting, and anything that hurts me as I am, at least, preventing further conflicts, especially at home.'
- 'I can fix problems between others if only I learn to behave.'

- 'I can rescue my people from suffering by behaving exactly how they expect me to, even if it causes my misery.'

Remember, they first learn these patterns at home, with their parents, before subsequently enacting them with friends, partners, or at work. So, now do you think that 'they better listen to me' is a good idea?

In all my interactions with parents over the last two decades, I know one thing for a fact—no parent seeking help wishes that on their children, so let's first explore the concepts of danger, parenting styles, and ultimately emotionally healthy parenting. Let's not lose heart; read on and see the way out.

A lot of times, parents expect their teenagers to follow their dictates, expectations, guidance, or goals without much ado or zero protests. When we encourage teenagers to do exactly what we say, unfortunately, we teach them to repress their instinct for autonomy and survival. They learn that they have to be a particular way to be approved by significant people in their life. They learn to be hypervigilant of our moods, our tones, and our reactions. In essence, they learn that love is conditional and the stability of moods that makes their lives secure seems elusive. In such instability and volatility, they try and escape by indulging in acts and relationships that are often self-deprecatory. Common examples include spending too much time on the phone or social media, prioritising friends over family, experimenting with alcohol, drugs, or unsafe sex, and so forth.

Creating a Sanctuary: Nurturing Safety and Trust with Your Teenager

There are two essential kinds of safety that every individual requires, not merely craves or desires on a regular basis. While we tend to be consciously attentive to the first type, the second may often elude our awareness.

1. **Physical Safety:** This includes everything that makes us feel secure, comfortable, and safe every day—all the little things that we take for granted and are easily available, such as running water, food, shelter, and electricity to specifics like a good locality, a safe home, money, a safe neighbourhood, and safe behaviours from those with whom we share space.
2. **Relational Safety:** People think that just because there is a blood relationship, friendship, or a close bond, safety is automatically built in. Safety in relationships is crucial, but we never pay it much heed, as we are not aware of what that means. It involves how a person's bids for intimacy or connections, like time together, values, or interests are received or rejected. It also boils down to how safe a person feels during conflicts or while voicing complaints.

We all need safe spaces to appreciate the good things we have in life. We also need safe spaces to express our difficulties, inhibitions, and failures. When we think of safe spaces, there is just one thing that we all have in common—it is about how emotionally safe we feel when we express ourselves that defines our overall sense of safety. When we do not feel safe, our fear responses kick in. They could be fight responses, like yelling, screaming, shouting, or flight responses, like not being available for interaction, or freeze responses, like being indifferent despite repeated reminders. As seen in the earlier chapter, parenting styles differ in their levels of control and demands, as well as in their levels of support and responsiveness.

Permissive parents are low in control but high in support. Authoritarian parents are high in control but low in support and responsiveness. Authoritative parents (not authoritarian) expect a lot out of their children (high in control) but also high in support and responsiveness. Finally, neglectful parents are low in both dimensions. The most positive outcomes in terms of children's behaviour occur when parents adopt the authoritative style. This means, for instance, that they show their children they care about them, but they also expect them to follow their advice and guidance—if for no other reason than to keep them safe.

Attachment and parenting style theories provide the foundation for attachment parenting as it's practised today. The parodies of AP either overemphasise the permissiveness dimension or regard these parents as over-involved from birth on up. What attachment theory and parenting style theory propose, instead, is that parents provide their children with a firm basis of support—a safe haven—and adjust their expectations and attention to their needs to the child's developmental level. That is the reason why when our teenagers act up, we can pause and think, could it be because they are not feeling as 'safe' as we think they are?

Dealing with Teenage Rebellion: Strategies for Managing Constant Protests

When children protest, parents often prefer to think of them as difficult, unmotivated, or not giving their best to tap into their potential. While this may indeed be true, let's take a moment to consider: What if there is another way to approach our outlook on teen parenting? How about measuring our parenting skills by the yardstick of raising emotionally healthy teenagers and adults? These are individuals who may struggle less in their relationships, achieve better work-life balance, and perhaps even experience that elusive happiness we as parents seem to be constantly chasing.

One useful technique to apply when dealing with a teenager who always protests, stonewalls, or is at loggerheads is to understand what we can truly control in the given circumstances. Unfortunately, it is not our teenager who is likely to change, no matter how much we desire it.

Sermons from parents may have been the norm for the current generation of parents' upbringing. Whether they liked it or not, they usually followed suit. But was that really a good idea? In therapy, I often encounter adults struggling with life challenges in their 30s and 40s, ruminating about how their parents never understood them or allowed them to express themselves or pursue their passions. Was that parenting approach truly beneficial upon reflection? Even if you answer yes, will it help you maintain or nurture those expectations?

Expecting the same approach to be adequate is akin to functioning without computers or the online world. While one may have been perfectly content growing up without it, that is not the reality for today's adults, let alone growing children. All parents have adapted to some degree to the online world, whether for social media use, grocery shopping, banking, or purchasing goods. Therefore, even if we believe that our parenting was adequate and our sermons are all our children need, the time has come to overhaul our thinking and enhance our skills in emotionally healthy parenting. Let's embark on this exciting roller-coaster journey. Let's fearlessly explore our role as emotionally healthy parents, ready to undertake the challenge of understanding the protesting teenager and willing to change ourselves while investing time in enhancing our parenting skills. So, are you prepared to thrive in this world of raging teen hormones?

To begin this process, assess your skills in healthy communication to become an emotionally healthy parent. Are you employing these techniques in your communication?

1. **Acknowledge:** Accept the other person's experience and feelings, even if you don't share them at the time.
2. **Wait:** Make sure the other person has finished speaking before you begin. Sometimes you might need to ask to be sure.
3. **Take it easy:** Don't rush into answering; instead, take your time. If necessary, ask for a moment to collect your thoughts.
4. **Sit back:** Acknowledge when you are becoming agitated and take a little 'time-out' to unwind—remind them that you will be back.
5. **Express gratitude:** When you end the conversation, thank them for their time, inquire about their well-being, and check if they have any further needs.
6. **Inquire:** Before engaging in a serious conversation, check to see if it's the appropriate time and place.
7. **Respect their decision:** If they respond with a no, respect that decision and ask when would be a more convenient time to talk. Ensure they understand the importance of having this discussion.
8. **Confirm:** Ensure that you are both relaxed and in a setting that is acceptable for a serious chat.

9. **Avoid blame:** Do not use 'you' phrases. For instance, 'You never listen to me!'
10. **Speak in a non-confrontational manner:** Employ 'I' statements, such as 'I felt wounded when . . .' for effective communication.
11. **Prioritise:** Concentrate on listening to what they are saying rather than planning your reaction.
12. **Make reflective declarations:** Reflect upon your own words and what you heard the other person say to ensure you understood correctly.

When speaking with people, we frequently concentrate on our next words. However, listening is more important for effective communication than talking. Understanding the words of the other person is only one aspect of listening well; another is truly comprehending the feelings of the speaker.

Emotional Maturity

The capability to comprehend and regulate emotions is referred to as emotional maturity. It promotes the development of a high-quality social and personal existence. The ability of teenagers to settle their emotions, together with emotional growth, independence, social adjustment, emotional stability, personality integration, etc., is another definition of emotional adulthood. Early life is the time between the ages of ten and nineteen. During this stage of existence, most maturity, which includes physical, intellectual, and social development, happens quickly. Emotional maturity can also be defined as 'the capability of adolescents to stabilise emotions including emotional progression, independence, social adjustment, emotional stability, personality integration, etc.'

According to the World Health Organization, the length of youth begins with the onset of puberty and ends with adult identification and behaviour being accepted. Emotional maturity is considered one of the main determinants in shaping an individual's character, behaviour, and attitudes, and it helps in improving relationships with others and enhancing the self-confidence of the individual. The survival of the individual in the modern-day scenario depends on how emotionally the situation is being coped with. As a result, emotional maturity plays a prime role in building the potential to make effective adjustments with oneself, family members, peers, society, culture, and the environment. The most exceptional mark of emotional maturity is the ability to endure anxiety, allowing individuals to tolerate the frustration they experience. A crucial indication of emotional maturity is that the individual assesses a situation seriously before responding to it unthinkingly, like an immature person or an infant. This results in teens ignoring many stimuli that could have triggered emotional outbursts when they were younger. The stronger a young person responds to the situation and their emotional reaction is closer to the scenario, the better and more emotionally mature that adolescent becomes.

According to Yashvir Singh and Mahesh Bhargava, emotional immaturity includes emotional instability. It is basically an individual's lack of capacity for solving problems and they will show irritability and always seek help from others. They seem to be more stubborn and usually showcase temper tantrums (Goswami and Roy 2019). The second category is all about emotional regression and includes traits like inferiority complex, restlessness, aggressiveness, self-centeredness, etc. The third category is social adjustment, wherein those with social maladjustment will lack social adaptability, harbour hatred, appear isolated but are always bragging, and are typically perceived as liars. The fourth area is personality integration, where people with this characteristic exhibit fears, phobias, etc. The fifth category is independence, where those who lack it appear to exhibit more parasitic dependence or an excessive reliance on others.

Adolescence is a crucial stage of life, and as such, it entails unique rights and demands concerning growth and health. Additionally, it serves as a period for knowledge and skill development, relationship management, and the acquisition of other traits and abilities necessary for both enjoying adolescence and fulfilling adult responsibilities. While adolescence can be defined conveniently by age, this stage of growth is distinguished by more than just chronological age. Every society acknowledges the transition from childhood to adulthood as significant.

Adolescence presents challenges, especially concerning emotional maturity. Adolescents may be impulsive, moody, and prone to outbursts of emotion. They may also struggle to manage their emotions and express them healthily. Emotional immaturity in adolescents may in various behaviours, including argumentativeness, irritability, and difficulty controlling anger, as well as a lack of empathy and poor social skills. Parents and other adults need to provide support, understanding, and guidance to adolescents so that they can understand and manage their emotions. With proper guidance, adolescents can learn to better manage their emotions and develop into emotionally mature adults.

The most important aspect influencing the lives of the current generation is parental encouragement. This is so that children can learn social conventions, first in the home and subsequently, in school. Parental actions are crucial for a child's future as well as for their current growth. The child's growth is hindered when they do not receive healthy family care. Parents need to be sensitive to their children's feelings and emotions. All throughout one's life, one should receive praise and support. A student whose parents never support them will not communicate their feelings, leaving them in a confused position.

According to Dr Kaur's research on the emotional maturity of adolescent students, parental encouragement plays a significant role (Kaur 2015). Parents are the ones who constantly support and wish for their children to be successful adults. Children get more self-assurance and vigour when their parents encourage them. Encouragement from parents is seen as a crucial factor in establishing a child's healthy personality. In the modern world, it has been observed that parents are often unable to provide for and create a harmonious relationship with their children due to a variety of family and financial issues. As a result, children often feel rejected, which impacts their temperament, motivation, and cognitive abilities.

Families play a crucial role in how well children do academically and professionally. According to Roe's hypothesis (1957), the pupils' occupational development is influenced by three different sorts of parental attitudes—acceptance, concentration, and avoidance. They adopt specific views about the family environment as a result of the attitudes their parents exhibit towards their children. There is a considerable difference between the emotional maturity of teenage boys and girls, according to a study by Sunil K. that looked at how the emotional maturity of adolescent students is related to familial relationships. The findings also portrayed a strong connection between adolescent adolescents' familial relationships and emotional development.

Adolescence is a period of intense emotional and physical changes, posing challenges for both adolescents and their parents. Emotional maturity is an essential component of healthy development during this period. Here are some ways parents can help promote emotional maturity in their adolescent children:

1. **Promote open communication:** Encourage your child to openly discuss their thoughts and feelings. Listen to them actively and sympathetically. As a result, they will eventually improve their communication and emotional intelligence.
2. **Provide an example for emotional maturity:** Parents must set an example for emotional maturity, as adolescents are more likely to emulate parents who manage their emotions in a healthy and positive manner.
3. **Promote self-reflection:** Teenagers need to have the ability to consider their feelings and actions. Teach your child to reflect on how their actions may affect others and why they feel the way they do.
4. **Teach problem-solving techniques:** Adolescents must be taught how to come up with solutions on their own and make decisions. You can support your children by assisting them in the process of problem-solving and encouraging them to develop their solutions.
5. **Support independence:** Adolescents should learn to feel autonomous and independent. Give your child the freedom to decide for themselves and make mistakes. Provide them with direction and encouragement, but also give them room to expand and mature.

6. **Validate their emotions:** When adolescents experience intense emotions, they need to be understood and supported. Even if you don't share their opinions, acknowledge and affirm their sentiments.

Ultimately, fostering emotional maturity in teenagers involves providing a secure and encouraging environment where they can grow in emotional intelligence, autonomy, and problem-solving abilities. Parents may assist their children in navigating the difficulties of adolescence and growing up to be emotionally responsible adults by offering them direction, encouragement, and validation.

The relationship between emotional intelligence and emotional maturity is significant. A person's emotional maturity and interpersonal skills—comprising empathy, social responsibility, and interpersonal interactions—are positively correlated (Arasteh and Seyedoshohadaei 2018). In reality, someone who is emotionally mature constantly works to review their emotions in a clearer perspective, postpones their expectations based on the need for a position, and achieves greater compatibility for strategy preparation. This person does not necessarily solve all the causes of anxiety and hostility, as fighting is more effective. As a result, they consider failure in a reasonable amount and respond to stressful situations by using their emotional experiences in the right manner.

As mentioned earlier, teenagers need an emotionally safe environment to feel at ease and secure enough to communicate their feelings and views without worrying about being judged or ridiculed. Teenagers' emotional safety area is largely created by their parents.

Here are some ways parents can create an emotionally safe space for their children:

1. **Establish Trust:** Building trust with your adolescent is essential for creating a secure emotional environment. This involves being dependable, keeping your promises, and maintaining integrity.
2. **Listen without Judgment:** When your adolescent comes to you with a problem or worry, listen to them without passing judgement. Instead of criticising or dismissing their emotions, validate their experiences.
3. **Communicate Openly:** Provide an atmosphere where your adolescent feels comfortable discussing their thoughts and feelings with you to encourage open communication. Ensure they know you support them.
4. **Be Accessible:** Let your adolescent know you are available to talk to them anytime. When they speak to you, be present and attentive to what they are saying.
5. **Respect their Privacy:** Honour their privacy and personal space. Avoid interrogating them excessively or in a way that might make them uncomfortable.
6. **Be Empathetic:** Try to understand your adolescent's perspective by empathising with them. Show empathy and awareness of what they are going through.
7. **Set Boundaries:** Establish limits with your adolescent and respect them. This will help them feel safe and trusted.
8. **Provide Positive Feedback:** When your adolescent confides in you, be encouraging and let them know you are proud of them for opening up and sharing their feelings.
9. **Seek Professional Help:** If you notice your adolescent struggling emotionally, seek assistance from a therapist or counsellor.

Case Study

Mainak was a fifteen-year-old boy who had always been known for his quick temper. He tended to lash out at others when he was angry, which often led to arguments and strained relationships. Concerned about his emotional maturity, his mother, Suchita, knew he needed help managing his emotions.

One day, Suchita decided to have a heart-to-heart conversation with Mainak. She explained to him how his behaviour affected others and emphasised the necessity for him ways to control his emotions. Mainak was initially defensive, but as his mother continued to speak with him, he started to realise that she was right.

Suchita decided to enrol Mainak in therapy to help him learn how to manage his emotions. Initially resistant to the idea, Mainak began to see the benefits of therapy as he started working with his therapist. Through this experience, he developed skills in identifying and expressing his emotions.

Suchita also worked with Mainak to develop a plan for managing his emotions. They created a list of strategies he could use when he started to feel angry or overwhelmed. These strategies included taking a break, going for a walk, or practicing deep breathing exercises.

Over time, Mainak began to notice a significant improvement in his emotional maturity. He was better able to control his temper and communicate with others in a calm and respectful manner. He also started to develop deeper and more meaningful relationships with his friends and family.

One day, Suchita was having a difficult day at work and came home feeling stressed and overwhelmed. Mainak noticed that his mother was upset and asked her if she wanted to talk.

Suchita was touched by Mainak's concern and grateful for the emotional support he provided.

As Mainak continued to grow and mature emotionally, Suchita felt proud of the progress he had made. Mainak's journey to emotional maturity is lifelong, but she was confident that with her support, he would be able to thrive and grow as a person.

11

Harnessing the Power of Humility

'Never look down on anybody unless you're helping him up.'

—Jesse Jackson

Society often associates certain values or attitudes with weakness, thus, as a rule of thumb, we never think about those aspects to have much relevance in our lives. Humility is one such word. Most people think that it to be a t heoretical concept, prized in scriptures but rarely useful in dealing with current challenges, like modern parenting. To add to their hesitance, visual depictions of humility are somewhat enslaved in mass media. However, that is not actually what humility is. Let's explore this concept further and dissect humility from the perspective of its potential for parenting skills.

Just as a clock needs all its gears to help us perceive time, in the midst of raging verbal wars or conflicts, we require all the help we can get to maintain control of the situation.

Parents often ask me, or wonder aloud, 'Wouldn't it be great if there was a master key or concoction of different ingredients to regain sanity and peacefully resolve conflicts?'

There is good news. Humility, defined by Charles L. Whitfield as 'a powerful attitude and a state of mind that when we are in the pain of conflict, opens us to more choices and peaceful resolutions,' seems to hold that elusive master key. It can be described through twelve basic characteristics:

- Letting go
- Openness
- Detachment
- Curiosity
- Integrity
- Patience
- Innocence
- Attitude of 'don't know'
- Tolerance
- Childlike Nature
- Spirituality
- Spontaneity

An effective framework for parenting adolescents is the framework of humility, as described in *The Power of Humility: Choosing Peace over Conflicts in Relationships* by Charles L. Whitfield. Humility is, in a nutshell, is 'having the openness to learn more about relationships.' It is a valuable virtue as well as an attitude that assists parents in healthy parenting, irrespective of their parenting styles. It involves being aware of one's limitations, being open to learning from others, and having a willingness to admit mistakes and apologise when necessary. Here, we are exploring why humility is a useful parenting skill and how parents can incorporate it into their parenting style.

Firstly, humility promotes healthy relationships between parents and children. When parents are humble, they acknowledge that they don't have all the answers and are willing to listen to their children's opinions and perspectives. This creates an atmosphere of mutual respect and trust, crucial for building strong relationships. Humble parents also demonstrate to their children that it's okay to make mistakes and that they can learn from them. This can help children feel more comfortable taking risks and trying new things without fear of failure.

Secondly, humility teaches children important life skills. When parents model humility, children learn the importance of being respectful, patient, and empathetic towards others. They also learn how to communicate effectively and resolve conflicts peacefully. Children who grow up with humble parents are more likely to develop strong social skills and have better relationships with others.

Thirdly, humility helps parents avoid the pitfalls of perfectionism. Many parents put pressure on themselves to be perfect, which can lead to feelings of inadequacy and guilt. When parents embrace humility, they accept that they are not perfect and that they will make mistakes. This can help them be more forgiving of themselves and their children when mistakes occur, and it can reduce their stress levels as well.

Below are some practical tips on how parents can incorporate humility into their parenting styles:

- Listen to your child's point of view without interrupting or dismissing them
- Apologise when you make a mistake or lose your temper
- Ask for forgiveness when you have wronged your child
- Model respectful and empathetic behaviour towards others

- Admit when you don't know the answer to a question and offer to find it out together
- Praise your child's efforts and progress, not just their achievements
- Don't compare your child to others or put too much pressure on them to be perfect
- Demonstrate meaningful and purposeful living if you expect it from them

Humility can move mountains and help us achieve our desired goals. A case in point is Mother Teresa, a humble nun from Kolkata who was recognised worldwide for her humility and selfless service for the destitute and was awarded the Nobel Prize in 1979. Humility gave her courage, a sense of purpose and determination to do meaningful work consistently, even in difficult times and in the face of adversity. Humbleness gave her fame, recognition, and applause even in an era where there were no public shout-outs or the presence of social media. Greta Thunberg's work in addressing the climate crisis is another example of humility in action.

Decades ago, children used to grow up on stories of *Panchatantra*, which had lessons on humility that were weaved into interesting stories. Today, most parents do not turn to this ancient wealth of wisdom that can prove to be a treasure trove of values. However, the ones who do, tend to reap rich benefits in terms of shaping their child's personality holistically. Reading these stories reminds parents to remain humble and practise what they preach.

Raghu is a 12-year-old who studies in a fancy school in Delhi and lives in a palatial house in Vasant Vihar.

Yet, his family's lifestyle is modest and simple, and they demonstrate humility in their thoughts and behaviours. Every summer, his family visits their ancestral village near Amritsar for two weeks. They all perform an active service at the Golden Temple every day, serving food to visitors, wiping the floors, and whatever else was required. Furthermore, everyone dressed and ate very simply.

Raghu and his sister spent three hours each day helping children at the local school, teaching them the basics of English, Hindi, and Mathematics. They also spoke about emotional intelligence with the help of simple books. His older cousin, who lived with them, volunteered with 'Teach for India' on a regular basis to help those who did not have the means for quality education, unlike them.

This is part of their family culture that Raghu, his sister, and his cousin adopted as young children. Raghu's parents did not talk about fancy brands or taking exotic holidays. Instead, they focused on character building and selfless charity with their own hands along with distributing knowledge.

Humility is a valuable skill that can help parents build healthy relationships with their children, teach important life skills, and avoid the pitfalls of perfectionism. By incorporating humility into their parenting style, parents can create a nurturing and supportive environment that fosters growth and development in their children.

12

Unmasking the Harmful Effects of Toxic Positivity

'You may give them your love but not your thoughts,
For they have their own thoughts.'
—Kahlil Gibran

There is an enormous amount of literature advocating the importance and benefits of a positive attitude. Gurus, teachers, and spiritual leaders promote the idea of maintaining a positive attitude because it is believed to be beneficial to health and success in life. However, positivity can become toxic when imposed on oneself and others (Fisher 2019). By forcing a positive vibe, we deny ourselves our true feelings and experiences. Toxic positivity is an over-generalisation of optimism and euphoria in all situations, denying immediate problems and suppressing unpleasant emotions (Quintero and Long 2019). This is because negative emotions are seen as unacceptable or bad, even when going through difficult situations, leading to the need to completely suppress them and force positive attitudes and thoughts. Consequently, some people resort to using different tools to stay positive. Some people employ positive assertiveness to achieve this. However, Wood et al. (2009) found that positive self-reporting is likely to backfire, especially for people with low self-esteem.

Additionally, a positive attitude can lead to inaction, even in situations that require immediate or decisive action. Sinclair, Hart, and Lomas (2020) found that an optimistic bias can be counterproductive when dealing with domestic violence. It can endanger victims and dissuade them from leaving abusive relationships. Toxic positivity functions as an avoidance mechanism, leading us to deny or evade emotional situations that make us uncomfortable. When faced with difficult emotions, we tend to ignore, reject, or deny them. Held (2002) expresses concern that positivity can foster self-deception by creating pleasurable illusions of oneself and one's reality, arguing that external events can burst this bubble. He warns that when positivity becomes toxic, it impedes our ability to confront difficult emotions and feelings, hindering deeper insight and enhanced human growth. The 'Only Positive Vibes' mantra can be particularly draining during times of high personal distress, such as financial hardship, unemployment, illness, and the loss of loved ones, as it may seem downright cruel to be told to look on the bright side (Cherry 2021). Berlant (2011) explains that positivity can be cruel because it can make people endure violence and despair by giving them the illusion that improvement is imminent. When you try to suppress negative thoughts and maintain a positive outlook, you push them into your subconscious instead of eliminating them. Wegner, Schneider, Carter, and White (1987) found that attempts to repress thoughts and emotions can lead to renewed involvement in these problems. When some thoughts are repressed, they can return to consciousness with minimal prompting and become obsessive pursuits.

Challenging averse emotional states like sadness and anger is a part of life. Adolescents need opportunities to build emotional resilience, which happens when they learn to perceive, process, and manage a wide range of emotions healthily. Unfortunately, overemphasising positivity in response to a child's negative emotions, such as 'Other people have it worse' or 'You'll get over it,' is not well-intentioned. Even if they do, they can unintentionally blame those emotional states, robbing them of important growth and learning opportunities for their development. Perhaps the excessive aggressiveness in responding to negative emotions in children and young people can easily be interpreted by adolescents as negative. If they feel like that, they may lose confidence that their parents will help them. This can reduce children's openness and communication about issues that will plague them in the future.

A growing body of research suggests that parental rejection of a child's negative emotions may exacerbate or escalate their psychological and emotional distress. For example, research shows that when parents overlook negative emotions in their children, anxiety, depression, chronic pain, and physical ailments increase. The explanation is simple: When children's distress is overlooked, emotional distress intensifies as they do not have the resources or support to deal with these feelings on their own. Conversely, when caregivers take the time to acknowledge their child's negative emotional states and be with them, their child's experiences and perspectives are validated, and their children perceive them to be supportive. Over time, it helps children overcome even the most difficult emotions. Research shows that teens whose parents support their children's negative emotional states by listening, asking questions, and reassuring them have significantly better emotional health.

What Is the Alternative To Toxic Positivity?

According to 'What Is Toxic Positivity and How does it Impact Kids?' (*Kiwi* Magazine), the main alternative to toxic positivity is acknowledging and validating other people's feelings and emotions. It can be as simple as asking how someone is feeling during adverse times or if they need support. Being a good role model is also an important part of preventing your child from falling into the tunnel of toxic positivity. Supporting friends, family, and loved ones who are going through difficult times in front of children sets a good example. Empathy and compassion are big buzzwords for listening and being with people. The key is to recognise their struggle and pain and empathise with it in a way that supports their situation.

When it comes to thought processes, optimism is one of the most important mental habits children can develop. Children who practice optimism are more resilient, less likely to give up in the face of difficulty, and interpret their experiences in ways that offer them control and confidence. Optimism has nothing to do with temperament. In fact, the habit of thought depends on how we interpret events, thus, it can be taught. Parenting is broadly defined as the processes or experiences instilled in a child that are essential for building self-esteem, self-esteem, and a variety of qualities to make what is called a 'good person'.

According to the World Health Organization, parenting includes important goals such as self-confidence, health, and safety, instilling moral and ethical values, affirming striving for growth, providing the necessary motivation and guidance, and preparing children for life.

As a parent, one needs to help their child understand the shades of grey that represent progress. To achieve this, point out areas where your child's efforts have shown small improvements and gently explain what else you can do to be successful. Whenever possible, parents should try to divide large tasks into smaller ones and teach their children ways to balance both the negatives and the positives. All children tend to view situations as 'all or nothing,' but this trait is especially problematic for pessimistic or toxin-positive children, as they perceive lack of immediate and complete success as failure.

Value of Optimism

Optimism suggests hope, but parents should teach teens that toxic positivity is rooted in denial of reality. Parents can achieve this by helping them overcome it. Rather than suppressing and shutting out difficult emotions, parents should help teens in developing healthy coping mechanisms. They must promote growth and healing irrespective of circumstances, and refrain from instilling guilt and shame for not being 'strong enough'. With patience and perseverance, parents can reverse almost any child's attitude. They can simultaneously teach their children the important value of optimism while helping them in acknowledging and processing their authentic emotions.

Case Study

One example that illustrates the potential dangers of toxic positivity among adolescents is the story of Sarah, a sixteen-year-old high school student. Sarah was a high-achieving student and athlete, but she struggled with anxiety and depression. She found it difficult to talk about her negative emotions with her friends and family, as they often dismissed her concerns with well-meaning but unhelpful phrases like 'just think positive' or 'don't worry, be happy.'

As a result, Sarah felt even more isolated and ashamed of her emotions. She began to doubt herself and her ability to cope with life's challenges, leading to a downward spiral of negative thoughts and behaviours. She started to skip classes, neglect her schoolwork, and withdraw from social activities.

Fortunately, Sarah eventually sought professional help and was able to learn more effective coping strategies. She also began to open up to her loved ones about her struggles and the impact of toxic positivity on her mental health. Over time, Sarah was able to build a support network of people who listened to her without judgment and validated her experiences.

This case study demonstrates the importance of recognising and addressing toxic positivity among adolescents. While it's important to cultivate a positive outlook and focus on strengths, it's equally important to acknowledge and validate negative emotions. Adolescents who feel seen, heard, and supported are more likely to develop healthy coping skills and thrive in their personal and academic lives.

Toxic Positivity	Genuine Optimism
Being negative won's help you	It's important to let it out. Is there anything I can do to make this easier for you?
Good vibes only	I love you through all your emotional states.
Yo'll got over it	You're resilient and your strength will help you get through it.
Other people have it a lot worse	You're not alone, and there is support to help you.

Toxic Positivity	Genuine Optimism
Crying won't help, just smile	It's okay to cry, we all do. Can I give you a hug or a tissue?
Just stay positive	Things are tough right now. Do you want to talk about it or do something light-hearted?
It's not a big deal, look on the brighter side	I know it feels like anything could go wrong. Let's think of things that could go right.

Let children think their own thoughts. Once they learn to be genuine, they will reap the lifelong benefits of authenticity. Fake behaviours tend to negate the innate self-confidence of human beings. It spells doom in the long run and is the root cause of a variety of mental health issues, including addictions and social difficulties.

Genuineness builds emotional strength and resilience. If we struggle, we benefit from tapping into our emotions to gain strength. We thrive when we build resilience by identifying our emotional ability resources (EAR). Authenticity helps us build our unique EAR. After all, only we know how a particular shoe pinches us and where; no one else does.

13

Unlocking Adolescent Self-Sabotage

'What is required for many of us, paradoxical though it may sound, is the courage to tolerate happiness without self-sabotage.'

—Nathaniel Branden

Adolescents are considered a high-risk category by parents, teachers, community members, and everybody in general. There is a general aura of fear about how they tend to be irresponsible and are prone to many damaging interests. Parents are constantly worried about their total apathy for their well-being as well as their questionable habits and mood swings. They feel pressurised and are constantly plagued by doubts about the future of their progeny—whether in academics or life in general. They keep trying to 'explain' to their teens about everything which can ruin them and yet, their words seem to fall on deaf ears. To improve their probability of getting their children to listen to them, parents must invest time in first understanding why teens seem hell-bent on ruining themselves.

Let's explore this concept of self-sabotage, and as parents gain an understanding of this important concept, they can invest in developing resources and thought processes to reach out to their teens. This, in turn, improves their chances of connecting with their teens.

What Is Self-Sabotage?

Self-sabotage occurs when we destroy ourselves physically, mentally, or emotionally, or consciously hinder our success or well-being by undermining our personal goals and values. It is 'insidious, profound, and universal' and presupposes negative thinking (Berg 2015). An example of conscious self-sabotage is choosing to eat cake despite the goal of eating healthy, which occurs when it is not recognised in the first place. People who fear failure may wait until the last minute to work on important projects, unknowingly avoiding potential promotions (Wignall 2020; Brenner 2019).

Another aspect of self-sabotage is cognitive dissonance. Cognitive dissonance is the internal imbalance or discomfort when words and actions are inconsistent with beliefs and values. When this happens, we alleviate our discomfort by changing our words and actions and redefining our goals and values. It seems unlikely that someone would intentionally self-destruct, but it is, and the consequences can be devastating. Chronic self-sabotage robs us of motivation, makes us sad and anxious, and hurts our self-esteem.

Self-sabotage is rooted in counterproductive thoughts such as negativity, confusion, indecision, and negative monologues. Perfectionism and impostor syndrome are also forms of self-sabotage. Insidious and ubiquitous self-sabotage is an ignorant distraction that prevents you from achieving your goals. Mindless distractions include binge-watching TV, surfing the web, scrolling through social media, obsessing over video games, and shopping online. Dealing with unproductive or destructive behaviour adds to unproductive thinking.

Common Self-Sabotaging Behaviours

Common behaviours include overeating, excessive drinking or substance abuse, pornography, smoking, gambling, self-harm, and excessive spending. Avoiding action puts one in a negative, self-destructive cycle. Common avoidance behaviours include procrastination, chronic tardiness, giving up in difficult situations, and lack of assertiveness. Rational fear is essential for safety and continuity, however, when fear throws us out of balance, it hinders our progress in our careers and personal lives. Common unfounded fears include fear of attachment, the unknown, change, failure, and loss of control.

Adolescence is a time of self-discovery and identity formation. For many young people, it is the time when the physical and the psychological clash. Teenagers can easily become victims of self-sabotage because they are under severe pressure or lack self-confidence. They feel pressure from peers, parents, teachers, coaches, and cultural norms. They feel the need to act, dress, and achieve in a certain way to be accepted at a stage in life where they lack experience and a strong identity. Two self-destructive behaviours often associated with adolescence are the internet and procrastination.

Today's youngsters grow up in two worlds, not in one. To the old offline world of traditional experience has been added the online world of the invention of the Internet—the greatest circus of human entertainment ever created, which is just a click away. Young people always face new evolutionary temptations. They can choose to deal with the tedious demands of responsibility, or they can choose to escape into the excitement of electronic pleasure. Therefore, escaping the internet can easily be a self-destructive method if it significantly interferes with important activities, such as completing homework.

Secondly, there are related work habits that are easy to pick up. This can be personally expensive. To enjoy the Internet, teenagers may put off repetitive requests that they do not like. Procrastination is a common form of self-sabotage. Because it is always a bad deal, they tend to buy freedom by adding requests later. Procrastinating leaves less time to meet demands, accumulating demands, and creating stress as an urgent incentive to finish production at the last minute.

Role of Self-Esteem in Self-Sabotage

One of the main reasons teens self-sabotage is their lack of self-esteem. This can have several causes, but the effect is the same. Feeling worthless, incompetent, unworthy of success, and even self-loathing are all feelings that fuel low self-esteem. Some teenagers engage in self-sabotage to feel in control of their situation. By sabotaging a situation and then rescuing it, they can boost their self-confidence in the short term. However, these 'rewards' have proven destructive in the long run. Low self-esteem can lead to self-destruction.

Self-esteem—these are two concepts merged into one. 'Self' is how we define ourselves, and 'appreciation' is how we value ourselves. When young people define themselves broadly and consider themselves friendly, they generally favour positive self-esteem and self-reinforcing behaviours. However, when adolescents define themselves narrowly, like 'I'm nothing but my problem!' and evaluate themselves harshly, like 'Whenever I mess up, that just goes to show what a loser I am!' they can engage in a pattern of self-sabotage. In doing so, they seem motivated to prove that they are powerless to define themselves differently and deserve the blame they give themselves. Helping such an unhappy young person usually includes broadening positive self-definition and appreciating themselves for the worthwhile person they are.

A deeper and more difficult problem that underlies self-sabotage is addiction. It is a deeply entrenched pattern of self-sabotage and usually requires support and help to recover. There seems to be an epidemic of teenage failures in school, teenage failures in success, and teenage failures in life. It is about how you can help yourself recover from self-destruction.

Parents are frustrated by this self-defeating and self-defeating behaviour. Teens are often too defensive to accept or listen to their parents' advice. What parents should do is not tell teens what to do, what to think, what not to do, and what not to think, rather than judging their choices and trying to draw empathetic and objective conclusions between the consequences of that choice. Teenagers decide whether to keep acting or try something different. This is often difficult because parents want to control their children's decisions but cannot do so. Parents must allow their teens to make their own choices, but parents should always present healthier and constructive choices to their teens, whether they accept them or not. Parents sometimes ignore young people's reactions to problems. But it is important to learn to process these negative emotions, so try not to ignore or ignore your teen's moods.

Mood swings when things go wrong in life are signs of healthy brain activity. Your children need to feel that you truly understand them, what is going on, and how they feel about it. Encourage them to talk about what is going on instead of just telling them to 'get over it'. It can take some time to accept difficult events that are out of your control, but acceptance can help you move forward. Feelings of pain, anger, and frustration can return from time to time. Be careful and see if your children are being too hard on themselves.

However, this reaction is normal. Teach them to accept those feelings and acknowledge that today is a bad day. But also remind them that they had good days and will have good days again. By encouraging your teenager to notice the positive occurrences in their life, you can assist them in accepting the changes they encounter.

Reaching Out to Adolescents

Accept responses with understanding, acknowledging that lapses and errors are natural. Instead of outright stating 'you are wrong,' recognise that reacting negatively to their responses discourages further communication. When necessary, gently redirect rather than bluntly asserting someone is wrong. Begin by calmly explaining your perspective.

Trust their reasoning and correct them gently, explaining your viewpoint. Parents often dismiss the reasoning of their teenagers, which can be reflected in their body language. Teens may react with frustration or disengagement, often mirroring the dismissiveness they perceive. Be mindful of your body language to avoid inadvertently conveying a dismissive attitude.

Be aware of protest behaviour that can arise when communication with children lacks the desired connection. Acting out in protest, akin to a baby crying for attention, only serves to widen the communication gap. Recognise the fundamental human need for belonging and connection with our children, understanding that our approaches to attachment may differ.

Lastly, avoid becoming emotionally overwhelmed by feelings of disappointment, anger, worry, or grief when faced with challenges in connecting with your children. Recognise these emotions and strive to address them constructively.

Parents often find themselves in proximity battles, yearning for their child's companionship and attention, while the child exhibits avoidance behaviour. With teenagers, parents often feel worried or frantic due to their unpredictability and need to create distance. As our fears grow in this unfamiliar hostile climate of connection, we tend to do everything possible to manage the unpredictability of our interactions with them. We may berate them when they are unavailable or do not answer our phone calls, feel angry when they are insolent and disconnected, and become overwhelmed with images of potential dangers when they don't return home at the expected hour.

This tension that parents feel is rooted in evolutionary theory. Since prehistoric times, being close to one's offspring guaranteed their survival. Our emotional brain, inherited from our ancestors, triggers a subconscious panic for their safety when there is a sense of disconnection with them.

However, despite our deeply ingrained emotional behaviours in relationships, the reality is that these are different times. Our teenagers prioritise forging deeper connections with their peers rather than with their parents, as their hormones drive their developmental focus elsewhere. Consequently, the more we pursue, the more teenagers display avoidance.

Parents must acknowledge that the challenges in parenting teenagers are not solely due to a lack of bonding but rather differences in the need for proximity, accountability, intimacy, and closeness. Understanding this helps parents communicate their expectations in a neutral or positive manner. When met with negative or indifferent responses from their children, they don't resort to protest behaviour. Instead, they can let go of their desperation and display secure attachment by remaining in a loving, compassionate zone, regardless of their teens' reactions.

By releasing their end of any tug-of-war, parents can foster more peace, harmony, and a climate of stable, healthy relating, even if there is distance. When parents exhibit secure relating, the overall interaction style feels safe and healthy, devoid of drama and regular crises. Using strategies and skills of healthy parenting enhances parents' satisfaction in their parenting journey.

Strategies for Communication

1. Refrain from putting them under the spotlight, as adolescents often feel like deer in headlights when our sentences begin with 'You.' Instead, consciously opt for a softer approach, using phrases such as 'I feel . . . when you . . .'
2. Enquire instead of demanding that they listen to you then and there. Begin your sentence with 'Is this a good time to . . . ?'
3. Use a respectful tone that they can imitate in the future. They will mirror you without realising it. Always—and this is important—begin your sentence with a soft and gentle tone. Gradually, the culture of communication will be one of respect rather than an exchange of diatribes and verbal tussles. Try it consciously for two months to see results.
4. Set a habit of weekly check-ins with your child. There may be times when points 1–3 do not seem to yield your desire to talk regularly. Check if half an hour can be set aside to talk every week. Set it at a place, time, and day that is convenient to them. At first, it might

feel like they're controlling you, but remember, you're showing your trust by letting them take charge of communication.

5. Choose to be open-minded and flexible. A tree that bends weathers the worst of storms. Being rigid closes avenues of communication. It is important to keep that in mind.

In fine, successful communication with teenagers requires a careful blend of empathy, consideration, and adaptability. Using gentle language, courteous tones, and consistent check-ins, parents can cultivate an atmosphere of trust and receptiveness. Embracing these approaches enables both sides to tackle obstacles with comprehension and strength.

14

Parental Burnout: Consequences and Coping Strategies

'To be a good parent, you need to take care of yourself so that you can have the physical and emotional energy to take care of your family.'

—Michelle Obama

Parenthood can herald the best of times, and it can lead to the worst. Being a parent is a life-affirming and deeply enjoyable experience, but it can also be life-denying and deeply frustrating. Parental burnout can develop when parents are chronically facing challenges and stressors without adequate resources to replenish themselves.

Parental burnout usually encompasses three dimensions:

- Chronic fatigue leading to overwhelming exhaustion related to one's parental role
- Feeling disconnected or emotional distancing from own children
- A sense of inadequacy and ineffectiveness in one's parental role

Dr Puja Aggarwal, a board certified neurologist and a certified life coach, says, 'Parental burnout is the physical, mental, and emotional exhaustion that one feels from the chronic stress of parenting.' It may be described as emotional detachment from your child, irritability, or being easily upset. Some people with parental burnout may experience forgetfulness and increased feelings of anxiety and depression, leading many to question their ability to be parents. Feelings of inferiority, confusion, and isolation are also common. Parental burnout is a unique and context-dependent syndrome resulting from prolonged exposure to chronic parenting stress.

Symptoms of Parental Burnout

The first and most important symptom is extreme fatigue related to parenthood. Parents wake up in the morning feeling exhausted when they have to face another day with chores or coping up with raising their children. They may feel a lack of finances, and pressure to role model and communicate. They feel so emotionally drained from parenting that contemplating their role as parents makes them feel exhausted.

Tired parents become less and less involved in parenting and establishing strong relationships with their children. Interaction is limited to only functional and instrumental aspects at the expense of emotional aspects. Another symptom is poor performance in parenting roles. Parents grow tired of parenting, become intolerant of their role as fathers or mothers, and no longer enjoy being with their children. Additionally, all these symptoms and conditions contrast with what parents previously felt about parenthood.

Consequences of Parental Burnout

Parental burnout is not spoken of even though negative thoughts are more common in parents than is believed. Burnt-out parents can be violent or neglectful towards children, even if they philosophically reject this behaviour. In an unpublished 2020 study, Annette Griffith found that higher levels of burnt-out parents who reported the syndrome also revealed higher levels of punishing parenting practices. It was also found that parents who reported the greatest change in burnout levels had the highest risk of child abuse.

According to Mikolajczak et al. 2018, there can be seven drastic consequences of parental burnout:

- Escapism
- Suicidal thoughts
- Addictions
- Sleep disorders
- Marital conflicts
- Partner-estrangement mindset
- Neglect and violence towards one's child(ren)

Parental burnout has different consequences compared to workplace burnout. Unlike at work, parents cannot take paid time off and delegate their roles to other children, much like how someone with work-related burnout finds a new job. It is so because burnt-out parents often feel trapped in their role and may experience more severe consequences than those who are burnt out at work.

In Western cultures, upon puberty, parents often worry about this developmental transition and assume it will be a difficult time. For instance, researchers in a somewhat older national study of Dutch parenting, conducted in 1996, found that parents viewed adolescence as the most difficult part and stage of parenting. These negative parental portrayals are often fuelled from the outset by mass media that tend to portray society, especially teenagers, disproportionately negatively.

They support some degree of positive parental expression, indicating that children can be a large source of stress and distress in addition to being an important source of joy and satisfaction. Once in, parents tend to face new challenges, like crossing boundaries, and various new demands, such as the need for greater independence and autonomy, which can lead to further stress.

The risk of burnout looms for parents experiencing extreme fatigue and lacking the resources to cope with the stresses of parenting. A confluence of emerging challenges and prevailing negative beliefs about young people can significantly impact parenting. Parents harbouring pessimistic beliefs about growth often exhibit excessive concerns about their children's safety, like susceptibility to peer influence, and health, such as engagement in risky behaviour. Consequently, they may become excessively invested, restrictive, and overprotective, adversely affecting their psychological well-being. Notably, research on parenting has predominantly centred on mothers, even when fathers are included.

The family structures concept serves as a framework to comprehend human functioning, emphasising interactions within one's family and between the family and the surrounding context(s). This concept has found application in various domains, including psychotherapy—working within a systems framework addressing emotional, behavioural, or relational symptoms in individuals, couples, and families—education, community issues, organisational consulting, leadership training, healthcare, and peace studies.

From a close family systems perspective, an individual's functioning is shaped not merely by intrapsychic factors but also by their position within the system(s), subject to the dynamics of the system, such as emotional demands, role definitions, boundary issues, coalitions, loyalty conflicts, cultural influences, and systemic tension. The interplay of self-correcting and self-reinforcing feedback loops within a system can either foster or impede pathology, health, breakdown, or resilience.

Bowen's family system theory comprises eight interlocking concepts: Triangle, differentiation of self, emotional process of the nuclear family, the process of family projection, the process of multigenerational contagion, emotional separation, and sibling position. In this theory, the triangle represents the relationship among three individuals, serving as the foundational components of a larger family system. These relationships are deemed relatively stable, as the dynamics between two people are deemed too fragile. The addition of a third person alters the tension and prevents the relationship from becoming overly precarious. Changes in the dynamics of the triangle occur frequently due to conflicts and tensions between its members. Although stable, these dynamics can give rise to various family problems. Within the family system, each individual possesses unique self-differentiation. Confidence in oneself reduces susceptibility to external influence. Confident individuals are less likely to impose their personalities on others. The development of self-confidence hinges on family relationships during childhood and adolescence.

Every family, much like society, comprises a mix of individuals with varying levels of self-differentiation—some exhibiting lower, while others, higher levels. Families have different degrees of emotional interdependence based on the self-differentiation levels of family members. The more emotionally dependent the family is, the weaker the members' self-differentiation. This implies that family units face greater difficulty adapting to stressful situations, as individual problems emotionally affect the entire family unit. A higher degree of self-differentiation corresponds to lower parental conflict and higher-quality social relationships (Gharehbaghy 2011). Empirical evidence also supports the link between discrimination and chronic anxiety, marital satisfaction, and psychological distress.

The emotional process within nuclear family consists of four relationship patterns that cause family issues: Marital conflict, spousal dysfunction, disability of one or more children, and emotional distance. These emotional processes can overlap, as marital conflict may create emotional distance, causing mothers to focus too much on their children and hider the children's self-differentiation. This explains how communication breakdowns can occur, and children may inherit various problems and strengths from their parents, with relationship sensitivity being a potent factor, encompassing a strong need for approval and a sense of responsibility for others' well-being.

Common parenting theories must adopt an ecological perspective, acknowledging that both interpersonal and broader environmental factors predominantly influence a developing child's risk or resilience. There is a growing consensus that the interplay of various factors across interpersonal and environmental domains shapes children's development. The ecological model posits that children's relationships with parents and caregivers are influenced by work, school, and community environments, as well as social, cultural, and political conditions.

Adulthood results from intricate interactions at individual, family, and community levels. Ecological frameworks study interactions between different systems crucial during childhood. Examining the relationship between poverty, health, social exclusion, and structural inequality's impact on families and communities draws insights from diverse research areas worldwide. Identifying, developing, and safeguarding informal social support sources for families in need is a vital task for social workers and welfare professionals. This knowledge, coupled with resilience traits in children and families navigating high-risk environments, guides effective ecological assessment and intervention strategies.

Historically, older people played crucial roles in supporting large families. However, contemporary challenges lead to skip-generation families, where grandparents step in as the grandchild's sole or primary caregiver when parents are absent.

Teenagers' relationships with parents evolve during adolescence, necessitating continued support. While parental roles shift from nurturing and guiding to more equal relationships, parents remain the source of care, emotional support, safety, security, and practical and financial assistance. Although adolescence brings ups and downs, family ties generally strengthen as the child matures.

Adolescence, marked by rapid physical and emotional changes, can be challenging. Peer influence creates stress, making the family a vital emotional anchor for the child's unconditional love and acceptance. Establishing rules, boundaries, and behavioural standards instils consistency, predictability, safety, and belonging, shielding children from risky behaviours and issues like depression.

Negative parental beliefs about adolescence impact how parents anticipate, perceive, and respond to adolescent behaviour. Longitudinal studies indicate that these beliefs predict worse parent-adolescent relationships and behavioural problems. However, the mechanisms through which these beliefs influence parenting experiences and stress are still unclear and require further study.

Descriptions of Burnout and its Impact on Well-Being

Recently, researchers demonstrated for the first time that parental stereotypical beliefs about adolescents—mainly mothers; 97 per cent of the sample—were negatively associated with parental well-being due to reduced quality of communication between parents and adolescents. Stereotypical depictions of adolescents in need of guidance and protection influence parental psychological adjustment by believing that storms and stresses lead to over-investment, restriction, or protection of adolescents during their growth. When adolescents encounter new developmental challenges and try to become more independent, overly concerned parents may become excessively overprotective.

In addition to being linked with negative outcomes for adolescents, parental overprotection is expected to have significant implications for parents, and may put them at risk for psychosocial difficulties and parental burnout. Sociocultural expectations regarding how parents should raise adolescents and shield them from the risks and dangers associated with adolescence can exert considerable pressure on parents to invest in their children's future and safety, possibly fostering parental overprotection. However, this may also lead to fatigue and parental burnout in some parents, as meeting such standards may prove unattainable. Parental burnout refers to a specific stress-related syndrome resulting from prolonged exposure to parental stressors.

Specifically, parental burnout is characterised by parenting exhaustion, emotional disconnection from the child, and a perceived contrast between the previous and current parental selves.

Waking Up Exhausted?

Parents with burnout wake up feeling exhausted and emotionally drained by the thought of spending another day with their children. They become less involved and function on the autopilot mode. As a result, they become less able to fulfil their role as parents and lose the satisfaction and joy of spending time with their children. Parental burnout, unlike workplace burnout and depressive symptoms, has specific and important implications for parenting—the risk of neglect and violence—because it is unique to parenting roles.

Recent studies have shown that parental burnout may be rooted in a tendency to over-invest in parental roles, and parental overprotection may be a risk factor for parental burnout.

Over-parenting, also known as 'over-parenting' or 'overprotective' parenting, occurs when parents tend to give their children whatever they want or desire, and when discipline guidelines are spoiled and non-existent. Parental overprotection can lead to burnout in several ways. One of the main reasons for parental burnout is the constant pressure and stress that comes with overprotecting their children. For instance, a parent who is constantly monitoring their child's every move or who is overly worried about their child's safety can experience high levels of stress and anxiety. This can cause physical and emotional exhaustion and make it difficult for parents to function normally in their daily lives.

Cycle of Dependency

Another way that parental overprotection can contribute to burnout is by creating a cycle of dependency. When parents overprotect their children, they may prevent them from developing important life skills and independence. This can cause the child to become overly dependent on their parent and can also prevent the parent from being able to take care of themselves. This can result in feelings of guilt, stress, and frustration for the parent and can contribute to burnout.

Moreover, parental overprotection can elicit feelings of resentment and anger in the child. Constant monitoring and excessive protection may make the child feel untrusted or disrespected, leading to frustration over the lack of independence. This, in turn, can give rise to conflicts between the parent and child and contribute to parental burnout.

Thus, parental overprotection becomes a risk factor for parental burnout due to elevated levels of stress, exhaustion, and resentment. To prevent this, parents should strive to find a balance between protection and allowing their children to develop the necessary skills for independence and self-sufficiency. Parents must prioritise their own well-being and avoid burning out while raising their children.

Impact of Parental Burnout on Adolescents

One of the primary impacts of parental burnout on adolescents is the loss of emotional connection. When parents are burnt out, they may withdraw emotionally from their children. This can leave adolescents feeling neglected and disconnected, leading to feelings of loneliness and low self-esteem. Adolescents who experience a lack of emotional connection with their parents are more likely to experience depression and anxiety.

In addition to these emotional impacts, parental burnout can significantly affect adolescents' academic and behavioural outcomes. Adolescents experiencing parental burnout may encounter difficulties at school and feeling unsupported at home. This can result in decreased academic achievement and increased absenteeism. Additionally, adolescents may exhibit more problematic behaviour, such as substance use, as they grapple with the stress and insecurity caused by parental burnout.

Finally, parental burnout can impact the overall well-being of families. When parents are burnt out, they may become less engaged with their children, leading to a decline in the quality of family life. This can have a ripple effect, causing a decrease in the quality of relationships between siblings and between parents and other family members.

Lastly, parental burnout can significantly impact the well-being of adolescents. It can lead to a loss of emotional connection, a decline in the parent-child relationship, decreased academic and behavioural outcomes, and a decline in the overall well-being of families. It is important for parents to recognise the signs of burnout and to seek help when necessary. By doing so, they can help ensure that their adolescents grow up feeling secure, loved, and supported.

Preventing Parental Burnout

Preventing parental burnout requires a multifaceted approach that addresses the physical, emotional, and psychological demands of parenting. Here are some tips for preventing burnout:

1. **Practise Self-Care:** Regular exercise, proper nutrition, and adequate sleep can help maintain physical and emotional well-being.

2. **Seek Social Support:** Building a strong network of friends and family can provide emotional support, reduce stress, and offer a break from the demands of parenting.
3. **Set Realistic Expectations:** Parents should not feel like they need to be perfect all the time. Instead, they should focus on what is most important for their family.
4. **Prioritise and Delegate Tasks:** Parents must delegate some responsibilities to others, including their children, and prioritise their time and energy to reduce the demands of daily life.
5. **Take Time for Personal Pursuits:** Engaging in hobbies or other personal interests can provide a much-needed respite from the demands of parenting.
6. **Practise Mindfulness and Stress Management Techniques:** This can aid parents in managing their stress and staying centred even in the face of challenging situations.
7. **Seek Professional Support:** If burnout persists, parents should seek the help of a therapist or counsellor to work through their feelings and develop a plan to manage their stress and well-being.

In summary, it is crucial to prevent parental burnout to promote a healthy and nurturing environment for both parents and adolescents. A comprehensive approach addressing physical, emotional, and psychological well-being is essential. Adopting self-care practices, seeking social support, establishing realistic expectations, prioritising and delegating tasks, enjoying personal pursuits, and incorporating mindfulness and stress management techniques are beneficial strategies. If burnout persists, seeking professional support from therapists or counsellors is key to developing a tailored plan for managing stress and enhancing overall well-being. Although parenting is demanding, prioritising self-care enables parents to navigate challenges with resilience, positively impacting the parent-child relationship and the well-being of the entire family.

15

The Art of Persuasion

'The mind is no match with the heart in persuasion; constitutionality is no match with compassion.'

—Everett Dirksen

Mastering the art of persuasion is akin to refining any other skill, such as writing, playing tennis, or learning a musical instrument. It demands patience, practice, and a deep grasp of human psychology. When dealing with teenagers, conventional methods often prove ineffective, as they possess a unique mix of independence and scepticism, rendering them resistant to To sway teenagers effectively, it's crucial to first establish rapport and trust. Genuine empathy and an understanding of their perspective are paramount. Instead of issuing commands or trying to enforce compliance, engaging in open dialogue and active listening is essential. By acknowledging their viewpoints and concerns, a foundation for constructive communication can be laid.

However, it is vital to understand that persuasion should not entail manipulation or coercion. Respect for your teenager's autonomy is important. Attempts to manipulate or pressure them into compliance may breed resentment and undermine trust.

Ultimately, mastering the skill of persuasion necessitates ongoing effort and adaptation. Every interaction presents an opportunity to refine your approach and learn from both successes and failures. By viewing persuasion as a cultivated skill rather than an innate talent, one can gradually become more proficient at positively and ethically influencing their teenager.

Effective Persuasion for Healthy Parenting

Jay A. Conger lists four essential steps for effective persuasion in *HBR's 10 Must Reads on Communication*:

1. **Establish Credibility:** Demonstrate to teenagers that they can trust you. Stick to your word and refrain from changing your stance time and again. This process is time-consuming but even if it takes weeks, do not lose heart. Remember, Rome was not built in a day. If your children learn to perceive you as honest, open, and trustworthy, the probability that they are willing to be persuaded by you increases manifold.
2. **Frame Goals on Common Ground:** Just as you would take time to make an important presentation at work, invest time in doing research and be ready to elaborate on why you think the way you do. Talk about facts that will appeal to them.
3. **Reinforce Your Position:** Being able to explain the shared advantages and benefits to them in a tangible manner is crucial for effective persuasion. For example, lollipops are strategically placed near the cash register in department stores to attract customers, particularly those accompanied by children, encouraging purchases.

4. **Connect Emotionally:** If you want to make your 'talk' impactful, pepper it with stories from your teenage years, metaphors, and numbers that you know would create an emotional impact.

I remember when my son was confused about whether to study or take a job after completing his undergraduate programme, a heart-to-heart conversation helped seal his decision. When I sensed that he was reluctant to pursue a master's degree at a prestigious university abroad, I narrated stories and shared my own experiences that had hindered my pursuit of the degree when I was his age. Furthermore, I elaborated on why and how I eventually pursued it much later in life and the impact of not doing so right after my undergraduate studies. I also openly discussed the tangible benefits of that degree for me and how I believed it would be beneficial for him to pursue it at that point.

The art of persuasion worked and created a win-win situation. It seemed to have worked as I was honest, shared tangible goals, and connected emotionally.

Cognitive Behavioural Therapy for Managing Challenges

I like to think of CBT as persuasion in action. CBT involves persuading our minds to think helpful thoughts instead of unhelpful ones that bring us down and throws us in a negative downward spiral.

CBT is an effective, easy, and practical resource for teens that can result in long-lasting changes in their mental health (You can refer to Chapter 8 for more information on CBT). The goal of CBT for adolescents is to support them in drawing connections between their thoughts, actions, and emotions. They get an understanding of their triggers and gain coping skills to alter their faulty thought patterns and alleviate their unpleasant symptoms.

Teenagers who use CBT can alter their ways of interpersonal interactions, circumstances, and overall life experiences.

Case Study: Ana

Ana is an 18-year-old girl attending the second class at the School of Fashion and Design in Bangalore. She has difficulties with motivation for learning and a difficult family situation. Ana was left alone with a mother who was constantly insecure about their future. She sent them the wrong and completely discouraging messages. Despite the difficult family situation and her lack of motivation, Ana continued to persevere and attend classes at the School of Fashion and Design. Due to depression, she was hospitalised at the local psychiatric hospital for children and youth and is undergoing medical therapy.

It was evident that Ana was listless and apathetic, and she avoided school when it came to tests and oral exams. Anhedonia, insomnia, negative thoughts, and a lack of appetite were some of the symptoms she suffered from. Following the beginning of treatment, Ana kept a self-monitoring diary (a journal) in which she recorded her daily activities, her related thoughts, and her level of anxiety after initiating treatment. Using a cognitive behavioural approach, the therapists used Socratic dialogue to teach the patient how to downplay negative thoughts. They then taught her to think more realistically and positively by utilising cognitive behavioural techniques. Ana's relationship with her mother has improved since using CBT techniques; they talk more, hang out, and even laugh together.

Case Study II: Rohan

Rohan was a 19-year-old and had recently been experiencing a lot of stress due to restructuring in his life. He had recently separated from his parents since he had left for university to pursue higher studies and was worried about managing his finances. In a nutshell, he felt that his life was falling apart. He visited a counsellor on the recommendation of his friends. He had been diagnosed with anxiety, and they agreed that CBT might be an option as he reported being anxious about everything and was unable to relax. On learning about the benefits, he decided to try CBT after completing his classes at university. In his first session, Rohan's cognitive behavioural therapist took a brief history of what Rohan believed had led to him becoming anxious and worried. She gathered as much information as possible about how he felt at the moment. The purpose of this was to identify unhelpful patterns, perhaps fuelled by persistent negative thoughts, which might cause Rohan to get stuck in a cycle of constant worry and anxiety.

In simple terms, the way Rohan's therapy progressed was by addressing the areas in which it was easiest to make changes. The process of changing beliefs, feelings, or physical states is not as easy as one might think, and it takes a great deal of time and effort to change those negative beliefs and thoughts. However, it is possible to make changes very quickly in our behaviour. By focusing on changes in behaviour first, Rohan was able to develop a new way of thinking and acting that eventually enabled him to make more lasting changes in his beliefs, feelings, and physical states. This was done by gradually introducing new ideas, concepts, and strategies that he could apply in his daily life. He was also encouraged to look at his negative beliefs and to ask himself what evidence he actually had for those beliefs, or if there were other ways of looking at his situation in a more realistic light. After his eighth session, Rohan reported feeling quite a lot better. He had developed a rhythm of exercise and social activity and found that his sleep was less disturbed and that he felt less angry and resentful. There was still a way to go, but he now had some techniques up his sleeve to put into practice by himself if he felt he was sinking into his previous patterns.

As seen above, persuasion works when there is a tangible solution and an effective benefit. So, let's elaborate on some of these practical techniques.

CBT Techniques for Self-Care

Some useful self-care techniques to counteract the challenges faced by young adults are stated below:

1. Locate the problem and brainstorm solutions as needed. Journalling is a simple and effective technique that can help teenagers locate and write about problems as they arise. A teen who journals can usually identify the source of their issues.

   It has been demonstrated time and again that one of the most efficient strategies for dealing with problems in daily life is to write down exactly what is upsetting them and lay out an effective blueprint to brainstorm and consider solutions.

2. Teach them to write positive self-statements regularly. Young adults can reflect on the unfavourable thoughts they employ to squelch good ones after identifying the source of their issues. It is helpful to write a self-statement to combat each negative thinking. The self-

statements they make for themselves should be kept in mind whenever they encounter difficulties, and they should be repeated whenever a negative notion starts to seep in. They'll quickly establish new associations and swap out negative thoughts for pleasant ones. Sometimes self-statements become too routine and need to be refreshed.

3. Looking for fresh occasions to have optimistic views. People who walk into a room and say, 'I despise that wall colour,' might train themselves to find five items in the room they like as quickly as possible. You can programme their phone to remind them to think positively three times every day.

4. Embrace disappointment as a necessary component of life. Life may occasionally throw one into disappointing circumstances, and how one handles them influences how quickly one can move on. Someone going through a breakup could place the blame on themselves, gain weight, and question the value of maintaining a nice appearance. Allowing oneself to experience disappointment while keeping in mind that some things are beyond your control may be a better strategy. Work on what you can control—jot down what occurred, what your takeaway is from the experience, and what you can do differently the next time—and be careful not to think too negatively. You may be able to move on and feel better about the future as a result.

It is difficult to overstate the value of parental guidance for young people navigating life. Parents can make a huge difference in everything, from helping children develop a positive body image and sense of self to confronting challenging behaviour from peers to providing study advice. The best methods to support their children are to talk to them about the things that trouble them, to listen, and to offer suggestions without passing judgement.

16

Supporting Teens through Stress and Unexpected Challenges

'We are what we repeatedly do. Excellence, then, is not an act, but a habit.'

—Aristotle

In the current times, everyone—including parents and adolescents—is open to mental health self-care and the importance of seeking help from qualified professionals when needed. Thus, in these open waters of receptiveness, achieving consistency, clarity, stability, and honesty while parenting is a strong possibility. Therefore, healthy parenting and sparking connection with your teenager is possible when parents make a habit of being supportive. Excellence in parenting is an art form, which can be mastered when practised repeatedly.

In adolescents, mental trauma and stress can manifest as obvious physical reactions such as crying or acting out, or as emotional or behavioural reactions, such as worrying or irritability. Reactions to stress vary with age and stage of development. Children, whether young or older, feel upset or have other strong emotions in difficult situations. While some react right away, others appear unconcerned at first, but show signs of turmoil much later. Each child's response depends upon their coping skills, genetics, vulnerability to stressors, parental guidance, and past experiences. The popular myth is that peer pressure, social media, and mass media affect children the most.

Yet, researchers often emphasise that role-modelling in the home environment is often deemed the biggest influence. How children react often depends on the way they perceive adults around them dealing with problems calmly and confidently. In these difficult moments, if they notice their parents and other adults dealing with any kind of issues in a calm and confident manner, they feel reassured.

When parents are mindful of the time spent on news media channels, there is less distress in both them and their children. But both the children and adults become distressed when they see repeated images of war and crime in the media. Thus, limiting news exposure is beneficial for everyone.

When parents feel confident that they have addressed all precautions for managing adolescent challenges, they appear relaxed and calm. They are then able to emerge as solid support systems for their children. When parents appear well-prepared, children invariably feel less stressed. However, it is important to keep an eye on children to see if they are more stressed than they can handle.

If you aren't sure how your teenager is handling stress, watch out for some or all of these symptoms:

- Returning to behaviours they have outgrown, like bed-wetting
- Excessive worry or sadness
- Binge-eating habits
- Changes in sleeping patterns or insomnia

- Appearing numb
- Increased irritability
- Angry outbursts
- Picking up fights unnecessarily
- Avoiding schoolwork
- Difficulty with attention and concentration
- Avoiding activities that were enjoyed in the past
- Sudden headaches or body pain
- Use of alcohol, tobacco, or other substances
- Restlessness
- Excessive crying
- Nausea
- Pins and needles sensation
- Rapid breathing
- Hot flashes
- Irregular heartbeat
- Increased blood pressure
- Experiencing changes in bathroom frequency
- Churning in the pit of your stomach

If any family member, especially children, is experiencing more than eight of the above-mentioned symptoms, engaging in simple mental exercises can be beneficial to alleviate mental discomfort and assist both parents and children in building resilience. However, if the discomfort persists beyond two weeks, it is advisable to seek professional help from a qualified mental health professional.

Ways Parents Can Offer Support

Parents have the ability to shape attitudes and patterns of actions that impact a child throughout their life. Parents are the guiding lights in their child's life. If the child feels judged, criticised, or unworthy, they shrink from their potential and develop a faulty self belief that they are not good enough. Therefore, making children feel supported and cared for is important to help children thrive and develop their potential.

1. **Unconditional Love**

   Children respond very well to unconditional love, especially, during a crisis. Parents need to move beyond focusing on accomplishments and let them be reassured by a non-distracted presence. Parents need to pay attention to what they are saying and not saying. They can affectionately point out mistakes if necessary and practise an attitude of 'letting go' for work not completed satisfactorily. The need of the hour is to live and let live.

   a. Focus on nurturing children's confidence and self-esteem.
   b. Provide them with space to safely explore ideas and play options within the constraints imposed on them. Encourage them to communicate openly about their feelings.
   c. A parent's smile of approval lights up the child's world. Reassure them by smiling and being open to listening and talking to them often. Parental attention helps build self-confidence and self-esteem.
   d. Openly share your vulnerabilities, and refrain from offering false assurances.

e. Resist the urge to assign challenging tasks to them. Setting realistic goals about what they can and cannot do will foster their self-esteem.
f. Be honest and transparent with your children, and don't hide failures from them. They need to understand that everyone makes mistakes. It can be reassuring to know that adults are not perfect.
g. Avoid criticising them, as criticism erodes confidence. In stressful times, criticism often feels constructive, leading to discouragement and tension in relationships.
h. Schedule fun activities by engaging children in enjoyable activities that can reduce their stress levels.

2. **Share Facts Responsibly**

Sharing facts responsibly with your teen is crucial for their understanding of the world. It empowers them to make informed decisions, nurtures trust, and helps them navigate misinformation. This cultivates critical thinking skills and promotes open communication, which is essential for their development into responsible individuals.

a. Keep them well-informed as information is empowering. Talk to them about the latest goings-on and give simple answers to their questions while sharing authentic facts.
b. Let them know that you have taken appropriate measures and reassure them about their safety. It's okay if they feel upset; share with them how you deal with your own stress so they can learn coping strategies from you.

c. Reduce your family's exposure to news coverage of current events, including social media. Children may misinterpret what they hear and become frightened by things they don't understand.
d. Set a schedule, as children thrive with routines. Even though their education and social activities may be different, having a set schedule can provide comfort.
e. Maintain regular routines and explain how they can help manage daily tasks efficiently. Discuss and create a timetable for chores, bonding time, hygiene activities, self-care, work, and leisure activities.
f. Go to sleep at consistent times and have regular meal times. This helps soothe the central nervous system and reduces stress.
g. Practise what you preach. Children often mimic behaviours they see, so laugh often, remain tolerant, actively listen, take breaks, prioritise sleep, exercise regularly, and eat healthily.

Mental Exercises

Mental exercises like mindfulness or puzzles help reduce stress by keeping the mind busy and promoting relaxation. Parents can help their stressed children by offering support, guidance, and teaching coping skills, creating a safe space for emotional well-being. Below are some methods you, as a parent, can ask your teen to follow:

1. **Deep Breathing**

   This involves taking long, deep breaths, as though from the stomach, and keeping the focus on the breath. In difficult situations, relaxation and breathing techniques are very helpful, irrespective of age. Some helpful practices are *pranayama* and deep breathing: Draw your breath in for four counts. Hold for two counts. Exhale slowly for the next four counts. Repeat this 10 times.

Any child old enough to count to four can learn how to do deep breathing exercises to lower stress. Children, with the help of adults, slowly count to four as they inhale, stop, and then count to four as they exhale. This exercise should be done for several minutes until the child is calm.

This exercise can be performed multiple times during the day. It is especially helpful before bedtime to calm frayed nerves.

2. **Visual Imagery**

This is a time-tested way for children to cope with stress. Children pick up the skill to create positive and relaxing images and thoughts. For example, they can learn about visualising a bright sunny day, playing in the park, splashing in the pool, etc.

It will help them to forget, even if momentarily, about the current stressors in their life. Over time, they will be able to use it to block upsetting thoughts and mental images. Another way children can practise this: They identify a favourite place, a relaxing point in time, or a special happy memory. Then the children close their eyes and imagine that they are at that favourite place.

3. **Talking about Stress**

   It is important that children understand why they are feeling the way they are feeling. If a child wants to talk about feeling stressed, listen to them. Talking about it makes children understand stress, and they then feel equipped to cope with it, as it releases mental pressure in children. Use books and stories to talk about stressful and everyday events.

4. **Playing Mind Games**

   Playing board games or solving puzzles sharpens a child's cognitive or thinking abilities. Puzzles engage the mind and make children move beyond the stress of looming issues and challenges. When the mind is engaged in meaningful problem-solving, it does not feel anxious about environmental stressors.

5. **Journalling**

   Journaling offers a safe vent to tackle stress. It gives them an opportunity, especially older children, to release their feelings about a stressful situation. A journal can be fancy and attractive or as simple as a plain notebook decorated by the child. Initially, parents can help children to write about their thoughts and feelings. Younger children can visually express themselves by drawing pictures. A journal is a valuable tool for children to understand themselves and handle a particular stressful situation.

Parents can empower children with valuable stress management skills. In this process, they also pick up beneficial life skills such as sharing, critical thinking, and independence. When children learn how to cope mentally with stressful situations, they are primed to grow up into successful resilient adults.

17

Parenting with Compassionate Love

'The supreme happiness of life is the conviction that we are loved – loved for ourselves, or rather loved inspite of ourselves.'

—Victor Hugo

The book *How to Hug a Porcupine: Easy Ways to Love the Difficult People in Your Life*, suggests: 'When porcupines are threatened, the porcupine will grunt, growl, and stamp its feet, all in an attempt to scare off the attacker . . . Human porcupines would probably be indistinguishable from anyone else, except for their reaction to any kind of threat or incursion.'

Is there a possibility that teenagers are usually difficult because they feel threatened, unacceptable, or scared, so they would rather get you to back off? Therefore, they resist your communication. Are your expectations of them realistic? Often, their difficult behaviours have roots in their inability to fulfil the expectations of parents. Since it seems too difficult, they abandon trying to fulfil any.

So, ask yourself, how does your teenager perceive you? As an adversary or a loving presence in their life?

We have grown accustomed to unrealistic expectations from our adolescents. The zone of proximal development suggests that children thrive when goals are achievable and their joy for learning remains intact. Neuroscientists often emphasise that chronic stress leads to mental health disorders and physical ailments. Therefore, it is important that we learn to parent with kindness and compassionate love. Creating a climate of love requires us to balance our hopes, dreams, and expectations.

Asking the simple question, 'What memories do I want my teenager to have?' is key to enabling healthy parenting. With an intentional mindset, parenting troublesome teens becomes possible with compassion, honour, and repair work. Prolonged stress wreaks havoc, leaving parents anxious that their lack of oversight may lead to laziness and lethargy.

Consider the image of a one-year-old who is attempting to rise and walk repeatedly, driven by the curiosity and thrill of exploring the world on their own two feet. At this stage, they have not yet been subjected to criticism for their attempts, and they have no fear of failure, allowing their curiosity and interest in self-development to flourish.

However, as they grow, the constant fear of failure or criticism steals their willingness to attempt new challenges purely out of curiosity. It's important to remember that curiosity fuels intelligence like nothing else. Thus, bringing peace and calm acceptance into your parenting is vital. Doing so will lay the foundation for achieving goals in their own minds.

Gut-Punching Moments—How to Handle Unpleasant Feelings

Imagine a scene: You have just narrated a joke to a group of friends. As you deliver the punchline, there's a moment of silence, followed by someone laughing and ridiculing your joke as lame. Others chime in. In that moment, how do you feel? It's a gut-punching moment, where unpleasant emotions hit us like a physical blow.

Typically, when faced with such discomfort, we instinctively recoil, as if we have been struck. Many of us try to navigate through these uncomfortable situations by minimising or denying the feelings, unsure of how to manage the flood of negative thoughts. Yet, it is worth noting that handling these feelings is possible through the cultivation of presence and the practice of a simple formula.

Psychologist Dr Joan Rosenberg emphasises the significance of the small, moment-to-moment choices we make to either confront or deny our feelings. Being aware and staying present with are feelings is a choice. We must check in with ourselves: What are we feeling? How do we cope? Do we distract ourselves subtly by tensing our muscles or swallowing hard, or do we resort to more overt distractions like substance use, smoking, vaping, or excessive shopping?

Ultimately, the willingness to be present is the choice we must consciously make. By embracing our emotions and staying grounded in the moment, we can effectively navigate through gut-punching moments and emerge stronger on the other side.

Below are eight feelings that are typically negative and unpleasant:

- Shame
- Helplessness
- Disappointment
- Anger
- Vulnerability
- Sadness
- Disgust
- Fear

There are two main reasons why we avoid these feelings: They overwhelm us, or we feel we will get swept away and lose control of them.

However, our emotional strength increases each time we are able to move through and manage these feelings.

When an emotional feeling arises, biological chemicals are activated, which is experienced in the body. That is what 'triggered' means. We want to feel our emotions, but the subconscious threat or fear of resulting discomforting bodily sensations stops us. Thoughts like 'I never want to feel that again' are automatically activated. Thus, the choice in front of us is always just one—say yes to the feeling or deny and supress it. The power lies in assessing if we are ready to observe and accept that feeling without the fear of the consequences of that particular feeling, getting washed away by it. Always accept this feeling, as the solution involves riding the biochemical wave that lasts for roughly 60–90 seconds. It then automatically dissipates as it moves through our bloodstream.

Waves on a sea beach could be tumultuous, moderate, or mild. Yet, the visualisation of a sea invariably calms us. There is always more than one wave, yet we aren't threatened by them. Therefore, we need to look at emotions in our minds as waves that will always subside. To surf those 90-second waves, what we need to do is to get centred, acknowledge them, and then ride them. Unhooking from the gut punch of unpleasant thoughts is possible. Each time we are fully conscious and 'present' with an emotion that we have labelled as 'unpleasant', we raise our emotional strength and unfurl confidence in our own capacity.

One interesting way such unpleasant feelings can be managed is through 'The Rosenberg Reset', highlighted by Dr Joan Rosenberg. It involves three simple steps to navigate uncomfortable feelings instead of avoiding them: 1 choice, 8 emotions, 90 seconds.

The basic idea is to empower ourselves by becoming aware of uncomfortable feelings rather than resorting to avoiding them. These three steps can help parents thrive and successfully achieve healthy parenting by learning to lean into uncomfortable emotions.

> Step 1 begins with parents choosing to fully experience their emotions, thoughts, and physiological sensations. This concept identifies eight primary emotions: Sadness, shame, helplessness, anger, disappointment, vulnerability, frustration, and embarrassment.
>
> Step 2 involves acknowledging these emotions within ourselves in any given situation. While avoiding these eight feelings may provide temporary relief, the long-term impact is disastrous. Emotions, when avoided or suppressed, create internal roadblocks that hinder success, communication, vitality, and growth. The mental processes and energy that could have been used to pursue fulfilment are instead diverted into maintaining bottled-up emotions, resulting in an ever-growing mountain of repressed emotional pain.
>
> Step 3 entails noticing changes in the body when fully experiencing an emotion. Is the face flushed? Is the mouth dry? Is the stomach clenching or the head spinning? Being attuned to one's body helps in understanding emotions. Feelings are experienced instantly at a physical and neurological level, before full awareness sets in. By being mindful of physical sensations, one can choose to regulate emotions at their onset. These physical sensations are temporary, and the body naturally relaxes from its aroused

state within 90 seconds. By tolerating discomfort for this brief period, the body automatically re-regulates, achieving emotional stability.

Thus, the Rosenberg Reset is an easy, effective tool for maintaining emotional balance. The end result is a relaxed, assertive parent who remains unruffled by their teenagers.

Common Challenges Faced by Teenagers

Every person experiences the crucial life stage of adolescence. While some approach this time with positivity and strength, others struggle with numerous issues. The milieu in which young adults reside—their parents, friends, living circumstances, level of education, and various other factors—all play a role. Teenagers grapple with a variety of issues, including drug and alcohol addiction, peer pressure, self-image and weight concerns, and even disagreements with their parents.

Among all age groups, teenagers face the greatest challenges. They are neither independent like adults nor as dependent like children. Many parents are unaware of the myriad challenges their teenagers encounter. These struggles include adjusting to new educational environments, persuading parents of their need for independence, and overcoming social problems.

The teenage years present many challenges, one being the adjustment to a new school environment. Adolescents notice the stark differences once they reach junior high, encountering enormous academic work. Many also struggle to establish identity during adolescence due to biological and social influences. Family and societal support may occasionally be of little assistance in alleviating this burden. Body image issues, hormonal changes, social and parental pressures, family conflicts, academic stress, substance abuse, sexual orientation exploration, and suicidal ideation are common difficulties teenagers experience.

Primarily, teenagers often struggle with body acceptance, experiencing dissatisfaction with their appearance. Environmental influences, such as media exposure, exacerbate body image issues. Some aspire to resemble the idealised figures portrayed in media, leading to extreme behaviours and potentially harmful consequences like eating disorders, anxiety, depression, and low self-esteem (Gregoire 2013).

Socially, teenagers may become overly self-absorbed, unaware of others' struggles, posing a significant hurdle in adolescence. Learning to exercise rights while developing a sense of morality is crucial. Teenagers must make wise decisions, considering the well-being of others to avoid harming themselves in the process.

Building self-confidence is essential for teenagers to explore their identities and bolster self-esteem. Many struggle with low self-esteem and feelings of alienation, necessitating healthy coping mechanisms such as participation in extracurricular activities or joining support groups.

Navigating relationships becomes vital during adolescence as well. Developing strong bonds with supportive individuals while avoiding toxic relationships is crucial. Effective communication skills are necessary for resolving conflicts amicably.

Additionally, teenagers must exemplify appropriate behaviour, demonstrating self-control, integrity, respect, accountability, cooperation, and teamwork. Learning to resolve disputes without resorting to force or aggression is essential. These skills are cultivated over a lifetime and are particularly crucial during adolescence, a period marked by significant changes, independence development, socialisation, and career exploration. However, adolescent issues may arise unpredictably, with some common problems including:

1. **Negative Body Image:** Teenagers struggle to feel happy in their own flesh as they transition into adulthood due to the changes in their bodies. When they look in the mirror, they often see a stranger staring back at them, someone who is gawky, gangly, hairy, and unknown after the cherubic child has vanished. The pervasive feeling that their bodies are 'not right' can have several long-lasting detrimental repercussions, even if it doesn't lead them to overexert themselves physically or make them ill.

   Sadly, parents unknowingly add to the negative body image of teenagers by constantly commenting on their weight, looks, or dressing style.

2. **Need for Community and Identity:** Many teenagers struggle to fit in society due to their want to be accepted by their peers for who they are. They deal with anxiety and insecurity as they attempt to complete one of the most significant tasks of their lives. They may also experience feelings of loneliness, alienation, and sadness when they are told that they don't fit in. The television programmes targeted at this age group normalise aggressive and violent behaviour, rule-breaking, bullying, and other negative behaviours. This feeling of not belonging affects every part of a teenager's life.

   Often, remarks from parents about the unsuitability of certain friends or peers lead to a lot of friction.

3. **Time-Management Stress:** The more mature children become, the more stress they experience in school because of the various projects to complete, tests to take, and social dramas to deal with, not to mention extracurricular activities. Dating and hanging out with friends present an enticing social horizon. Parents tend to disapprove of the time their child spends on the phone, in co-curricular activities, and socialising, leading to arguments. Teenagers feel pressurised to balance all these demands. To add to their woes, parents often expect their teen to behave like an adult. They are expected to manage their workload autonomously, come to sound conclusions and act upon them, be great at time management, and even take care of their financial affairs and start planning their careers accordingly. All these expectations cause a complete breakdown in channels of communication between them.

4. **Popularity Pressure:** Parents often expect their children to achieve everything they had once desired but were unable to due to lack of resources. This vicarious living of parents is dangerous for teenagers, as it puts a lot of pressure on the teenager to do well in school, have great friends, thrive in extracurricular activities, and be responsible for both themselves and, occasionally, their younger siblings. Additionally, there is immense peer pressure as well because they are expected to conform to the likes, habits, and looks of their classmates to become 'popular'. The pressure further increases when the teenager feels that everyone around them is trying to change who they are—parents, instructors, grandparents, siblings, friends, classmates, and social

organisations all have an impact on teenagers and tug them in various directions.

5. **Lack of Positive Role Models:** It is often the case that the worst bullies, wealthiest spoiled brats, and most destructive children are elevated as the most admirable and popular. These individuals are exalted by the media and their depravity is celebrated in media like music, sports, and movies. Everywhere they go, our children are exposed to bad role models, and they pick up the corrupt standards of these so-called heroes.

   Constant fights between parents is also a regular feature in most households. In such a hostile environment, peppered with resentment or blame games, children can't find a positive role model around them. When parents disapprove or constantly explain how to improve, teenagers tend to rebel.

6. **Drugs and Alcohol:** The appeal, social acceptance, and addictive nature of various mood-altering substances entice many youths. Many a time, parents, too, are fine with frequent social drinking, unknowingly promoting a culture of drinking. Specific substances like marijuana and alcohol can harm a teenager's developing brain, yet parents often think that their own use of party drugs or alcohol is reasonable and will have no detrimental effects as long as their intake is balanced. Unfortunately, research shows that this casual attitude may be quite dangerous. One in four alcohol users has a genetic propensity towards alcoholism and substance abuse, therefore, encouraging children is never a good idea. It's essential to communicate with them to understand

what's happening in their school, with their friends, and the risks they face.

Instead of preaching to teenagers about what is good for them, what is actually helpful for their growth and personal development is learning effective soft skills. These skills help us in managing difficult emotions on a regular basis. Parents can facilitate the learning of these skills rather than moralising if they aim to become champions of healthy parenting and reap the benefits of good parenting.

Some of the soft skills that you can teach your teenager are:

- Self-love
- Developing internal control
- Ownership
- Collaboration
- Personal responsibility
- Creativity
- Self-advocacy
- Compassion
- Problem solving
- Time management

Love must be an action, not just a feeling. Parents demonstrate compassion for teenagers when they embrace their own growth and learning. The focus is on self-improvement to enhance communication and overall connection with teenagers. This proactive approach aids parents in evolving and becoming mentally equipped to navigate challenging teen mindsets. Parents who consciously invest time in developing their soft skills and resetting their mindset reap tangible benefits. They are perceived by teenagers as 'stoic yet loving and approachable.' The parent who diligently follows this path will undoubtedly experience the Eureka moment of 'I finally understand my teenager's perspective!'

18

Exploring the Essence of a Good Parent-Teen Relationship

'What's More Important: Your Ego or Hearing Your Child?'

—C. Lynn Williams

Parents of teenagers are discovering that their children not only look like adults but think like them, too. However, people agree that adolescents think more progressively, efficiently, and effectively than younger children. During puberty, they become more capable of reasoning about things that are more abstract and hypothetical than children. There are also advances in 'metacognition' as adolescents begin to think about the thought process itself. Eventually, adolescents' thinking becomes more multidimensional and relativistic. Like the physical changes of adolescence, the cognitive changes, too, upset the balance that parents and children previously established.

Adolescents introduce new cognitive perspectives into family discussions, decision-making, and debates, thereby challenging the way families address issues and reach decisions. As children develop cognitive abilities, they may want to be treated like adults and have more say in making decisions. This reorganised balance allows parents to recognise their adolescent's cognitive enhancement and remaining intellectual limitations, gradually increasing their decision-making opportunities.

Ultimate Well-Being of Adolescents

One of the most common themes in parent-child relationship is the direct association between positive outcomes for children and the quality of relationships between parents. Therefore, it can be said that the ultimate well-being of adolescents depends much more on parenthood than previously established. Several variables influence parenthood, ranging from behavioural patterns to socioeconomic details. A child's externalisation and internalisation, or instances of inadequate competence, can thus be viewed as important factors in the development of certain emotions and behaviours.

Numerous factors come to the fore when considering what a good parent-child relationship should entail. Researchers often refer to the types of bonds that bind compounds together to describe the overall concept of bonding. Other factors considered in such a relationship include good communication between the two and whether the relationship is maintained with the help of care. Consequently, individuals often face many negative consequences during childhood, adolescence, or even adulthood (Steele and McKinney 2018). Previous research has shown that children who have good relationships with their parents are less likely to engage in violence at some point in their lives.

Parenting is considered one of the most fulfilling roles a person can undertake. However, it comes with its set of challenges, and it is important to adapt or develop strategies to mitigate these challenges. Modern family life is stressful, and the pressure is not easy for most parents. Parent-child relationships are determinants of a child's emotional, social, and physical development (Steele and McKinney 2018).

A unique bond is formed in the process, and both parties enjoy each other's company. Positive parenthood is crucial in laying the foundation for life choices, personality traits, and general behaviour. It also enhances mental, physical, and emotional health. Studies examining some of the factors that contribute to the development of healthy relationships between parents and children have found that young children who grow up in healthy homes and with secure parental attachments are more likely to develop healthy relationships later in life. They conclude that these children are more likely to have satisfying and happy relationships. Additionally, children with strong connections also learn to manage their emotions when facing stressful situations.

Deviant Behaviour

When the parent-child relationship is studied in terms of the child's potential for deviant behaviour, then faulty or absent role modelling holds many answers. Children learn positive elements of society when they have nurturing and healthy relationships with family members as well as with people of the same age group.

Children who receive parental guidance and encouragement are less likely to engage in criminal activity against people as they grow up to value community responsibility and believe in living with rules and norms laid out for everyone's well-being in the community.

However, children are more likely to become involved in criminal behaviour in situations where there is no attachment with the parents. One component of deviant behaviour involves violent behaviour that has been meted out to them during their formative stage. Hirschi's Social Bond Theory can be used to explain certain potholes in the relationship between children and their parents. Delinquent behaviours in adolescents can be understood when viewed from the lens of this theory.

According to a report by the Office of Justice Programs, 'Hirschi's social control theory suggests that delinquent adolescents fail to develop societal bonds consisting of (1) attachment to parents, peers, and school; (2) occupational and educational commitment; (3) academic involvement; and (4) belief in social rules and convention.'

Hirsch argues that socialisation and the formation of personal relationships with peers and family members are some of the most important factors in human development that deter individuals from engaging in criminal activity.

Social attachment theory states that it is through such attachment that children find themselves dependent on others and in need of empathy as they pick up societal rules. For instance, if you go against social norms and age, you will be punished, such as going to prison. In this study, the relationship between parents and children can be viewed in terms of beliefs and attachment relationships. Additionally, this theory can be used to show how young people are affected in their communities when they cut off family ties.

Navigating Difficult Paths

Parents may find that adolescents view social conventions and moral standards in a more relative way, in addition to changes in how they approach decision-making. Adolescents' perceptions of the subjectivity of social conventions and moral norms may be accompanied by phases of temporary conflict.

During adolescence, rules are challenged as young people begin to realise that moral standards and social conventions are subjective, sometimes arbitrary, and may cause quarrels over worldly issues that are common in homes with adolescents.

When teenagers and parents discuss clothing, curfews, or tattoos, each may define the issue differently. Parents may view these as questions of 'right' or 'wrong' according to social norms. Adolescents, on the other hand, tend to define the same question as a matter of personal choice.

Judith Smetana believes that teens and their parents often argue about definitions rather than details of issues. Disputes are fought over who has the power and whose jurisdiction is at stake (Smetana 1995).

As a result of normal cognitive development, children who are willing to accept their parents' views on right and wrong and who do not question their parents when they say, 'We don't leave our clothes on the floor,' grow into compliant adolescents. Parents also tend to be more tolerant and indulgent. They overlook some issues as personal choices rather than unnecessarily getting ruffled. This results in an overall harmonious and supportive environment at home for all family members.

Importance of Redefining the Teen-Parent Relationship from the Lens of Separation-Individuation

According to a 2015 research paper (Aslan and Gelbal 2016), 'Separation-individuation is redefining the relationship between an individual and their caregivers such as mother and father by means of moving away from this dependency on parents on their way to independence and autonomy. It is expected that adolescents separate from their parents with the help of physical, mental, interpersonal and emotional developments during separation-individuation process.'

The process of individuation is characterised by mental rejection of parental control. Much of the process is in the mind, i.e., cognitive, rather than behavioural. Successful individuation is not necessarily accompanied by overt rebellion or opposition. In simple terms, everyday discussions and arguments between adolescents and their parents reflect the adolescents' inner turmoil as they negotiate this internal process of individuation of 'I am here.'

Although the theoretical healthy end of this model is individuation rather than separation, the bottom line is that successful individuation rarely happens without creating ripples of anarchy and discomfort as the domestic power dynamics gift. The truth is that parent-adolescent conflict is the primary mechanism for changing relationships. Moreover, the emerging new equilibrium involves more 'separated' adolescents who have rejected their parents—not only in a cognitive or mental sense but also in terms of day-to-day lifestyles, priorities, life goals, social activities and working values.

Since the late 1970s and early 1980s, models of adolescent-parental relationships have recognised the need for adolescents to individualise and develop emotional autonomy. A healthy approach to parenting at this juncture is acknowledging the transformation and easing comfortably into the changing power dynamics. This adaptability and matured outlook creates a new balance, wherein healthy, individualised (responsible, independent, and capable) adolescents enjoy warm and intimate relationships with parents that gradually accept and facilitate the gradual increase in the adolescent's autonomy.

One of the most important predictors of specific behaviour is attachment to parents (refer to Chapter 3 for attachment styles) or significant others. Whether parents are ready or not, this progress towards individuation is something that cannot be changed.

Healthy parenting is viewed through the prism of engaging in behaviours that affect well-being, whether positively or negatively. This lens is especially useful when addressing concerns in parent-child relationships, as intimate and social ties regulate human well-being and behaviour.

Ways to Create a Healthy and Supportive Environment for Teenagers

Businessman and New York Times bestselling author Gary Vaynerchuk writes in his book *Twelve and a Half*, 'Every single person who has a child is a leader . . . The growth potential . . . is limited by the emotional intelligence of leaders . . .'

Parenting adolescents can be a challenging task, as they go through a period of significant physical, emotional, and cognitive changes. However, there are several strategies—mentioned below—that parents can use to create a healthy and supportive environment for their teenagers.

Active Listening

It is crucial for parents to maintain open and honest communication with their adolescents. This means actively listening to their concerns without instantly jumping in with solutions and what they 'should' do. However, wait for them to reach out to you. Even when they do come up to you, be willing to explore the topic of discussion further with them. Asking open-ended questions with words like how, when, and what are helpful to deep dive into the issue with them. This builds trust and shows them that you are ready to talk, even offer guidance and support, without the tyranny of 'shoulds'—this concept was proposed by German psychoanalyst Karen Horney. This helps teenagers develop the soft skills of self-awareness and curiosity, while making sure that their innate emotional intelligence flourishes, paving the way for eventual success and happiness.

Balance

It is also important for parents to set clear boundaries and expectations for behaviour, while also being flexible and understanding of the unique challenges that adolescents face. It is often said that children need positive reinforcement just like how fish needs water. However, be willing to have difficult conversations along with offering honest and critical feedback when essential. At the same time, it is important to be candid with them, but make sure to be kind.

However, *only* positive reinforcements make it worse, as they lead to disillusionment and a sense of grandiosity. The faulty thinking of 'I, me, myself, and the rest can go to hell' is counterproductive to healthy functioning and creates a sense of entitlement, leading to a breakdown in relationships.

Charity

It is a virtue that has been celebrated since ancient times. The five concrete benefits of charity include nurturing gratitude, creating social connections, promoting a feeling of abundance, spreading joy, and serving as a surefire prescription to make us happy. While being centred in the self is a good practice as it means maintaining our equilibrium, despite life's ups and downs. However, most people tend to take a literal and surface-level approach to the concept of being centred in the self, interpreting it to mean that it's okay to gratify one's own desires at any cost. This kind of thinking creates a false sense of bravado and, over time, tends to make us irresponsible and leads to several social and interpersonal challenges.

Humanity

It encourages us to look after ourselves and our needs but also to do our bit in making the world a better place for fellow human beings. Being human helps us develop a strong sense of connection with people in society. It provides us with an opportunity to live a meaningful life and reach out to the most vulnerable. Human beings thrive due to interdependence. History is proof that for both the great ancient civilisations, like the Mayans, and remote tribal societies, interdependence was key for growth. When we realise that, for the sake of the survival of our shared humanity, it is imperative not to be self-centred, we automatically pave the way for these values to be absorbed by our teenagers.

Be a Changemaker

Each one of us can make a difference and change the world, even slightly, in which we live. Selfishness seeks gratification at any cost, creating isolation over time and a sense of void within. It is important to balance self-gratification with regular community service or giving back to society in any way that brings sustainable growth and development for the upliftment of society. Adapting and changing one's own mindset, by developing the skill set for an aquatic lifestyle, has been beautifully depicted in the movie Avatar 2.

Fostering Independence and Autonomy

Parents tend to resist independent thinking as it threatens their sense of control over their growing children. They consciously or subconsciously resist change, even though some concepts like online studying was foreign to them but the norm for the teens. Pre-pandemic, only a few parents supported online research for studies. Most parenting issues centred around the time that teenagers spent on their phones, claiming to do research. While it is a moot point on what was happening, the unforeseen impact of the pandemic changed that resistance to online education, despite continued reservations on the impact of screen time. What we need is conversations about the pros and cons of screen time and coming to a consensus on what is feasible.

This can be achieved by encouraging teens to take on responsibilities, make their own decisions, and solve their own problems. Another bone of contention is the need for teenagers to lock their doors or insist on not sharing details of what they do with their friends. Parents who acknowledge their teenager's need for privacy and personal space tend to have greater rapport and less parenting stress.

Conclusively, healthy parenting is possible. By understanding their adolescent children, providing them with support and guidance, setting clear expectations and boundaries, and helping them pursue their interests, parents can assist in their children's development into responsible adults. Effective parenting of adolescents is important for their healthy development, providing them with the skills and resources necessary for successful and fulfilling.

It is essential that parents are also aware of any signs of mental health issues and provide appropriate support and resources. Additionally, parents can help adolescents develop a sense of identity and self-worth by encouraging them to explore their interests and talents and by praising them for their accomplishments. Nurturing healthy relationships and helping adolescents build resilience in the face of adversity also contribute to developing a positive self-image.

Furthermore, when parents are aware of potential risks adolescents may face, such as bullying, substance abuse, and risky sexual behaviour, they can educate themselves about these issues and be prepared to intervene if necessary. Providing a safe and stable home environment is crucial for healthy parenting, including maintaining a consistent routine, offering nutritious meals and snacks, and promoting physical activity and healthy habits. Teenagers who are encouraged to express themselves and their opinions become well-rounded individuals capable of independent thinking, thereby developing wisdom as a foundation for their values and decision-making.

As underlined repeatedly throughout this book, it is essential for parents to role-model healthy behaviour and attitudes if they wish to instill these qualities in their growing children. This includes demonstrating healthy communication, problem-solving, and conflict resolution skills.

Lastly, parenting adolescents can be challenging, but with open communication, promoting independence, providing a safe and stable environment, modelling healthy behaviour, cultivating a positive self-image, and being aware of potential risks, parents can create a healthy and supportive environment for their teenagers.

19

Parenting Master Key: Repair Attempts

'My heart full of gold veins, instead of cracks.'
—Leah Raeder

A popular Japanese art form called Kintsugi is an apt metaphor for parenting repair attempts. Psychologist and author Rick Hanson suggests, 'Relationships shrink to the size of the field of repair . . . But a bid for a repair is one of the sweetest and most vulnerable and important kinds of communication that humans offer to each other.'

Any verbal, physical, or another kind of comment or action that aims to defuse tension and prevent a dispute from spiralling out of hand is considered a repair attempt. There may be multiple disagreements between a parent and child every day, and there may be occasions when parents become too anxious or irritated with their child. Children may experience severe distress when a parent snaps at them or otherwise expresses their rage, leaving them feeling besieged, uneasy, depressed, overpowered, confined, and confused. Consequently, until trust has been rebuilt, children will probably be extremely anxious about future disagreements.

Disagreement isn't appealing to most people, especially when it involves someone we love and care about. Regrettably, disagreements often arise in relationships, particularly between parents and children. Parent-child conflict is a reason for families to seek treatment. To help resolve these issues, both parties need to be able to understand that repair attempts create a family culture where expressing feelings and opinions is safe, without fear of judgment or criticism.

With the help of open communication and mutual respect, parents and children can restore trust and understanding between each other, allowing for healthier relationships. Conflict within the family is frequently described by parents and children as stressful, unpleasant, and upsetting. It is challenging because it often leaves both parties emotionally drained, hurt, and wary of continuing their relationship healthily. Unresolved disagreements and the feelings that accompany them can persist for days or weeks and affect other family ties.

Families often strive to end all conflict, as it is seen as a sign of a healthy family dynamic and allows for different points of view to be heard and discussed. However, families may try to end all conflict to maintain harmony and peace. Parents may occasionally adopt a lenient parenting style with lax boundaries, rules, and punishments because they don't want to start a fight. For instance, a family may decide not to enforce a curfew for their teenage children to prevent an argument, even though they know it might not be in their children's best interest. For children, this can result in anxiety or a desire to appear flawless in an effort to minimise the consequences of the conflict. In either case, these tactics are likely to produce negative dynamics and long-term issues.

A healthy relationship is ultimately determined less by the frequency of conflict and more by the repair solutions each person utilises and is receptive to receiving. While it is usually ideal to use healthy communication techniques to limit conflict to a minimum, that is often not the case in most households, despite the good intentions of parents. The saying 'The road to hell is paved with good intentions' is apt when considering the defining underbelly of the ethos of conflicts.

When a parent expresses anger at their child, the child is likely to feel the full impact of that anger. This can lead to a vortex of heated interactions that often spiral out of control. In the aftermath, there is usually a dire need for significant conscious repair work, which may involve fractured communication, growing distance, and breakdowns. When repair work is neglected, knots in relationships can form. When this occurs, it frequently comes as quite a shock to both the teenagers and the parents. Both parties may feel disoriented and struggle to re-establish contact. If the damage is not fixed, the teenager could unknowingly create coping mechanisms in the form of defences. However, they pay a significant price for it in other parts of their lives. For example, they might be less prone to confiding in their parents, feel generally more agitated, struggle to learn how to be patient in relationships in general, or suffer from low self-esteem.

Repair attempts are described by John Gottman, PhD, as a secret weapon of emotionally competent human beings in his book *The Seven Principles for Making Marriage Work*. In my practical experience as a therapist, I have often found this framework quite useful. What helps in fixing a marriage works very well when it comes to unravelling parental knots and breakdowns.

Dr Gottman's groundbreaking research demonstrates that one of the key determinants of whether a relationship will succeed or fail is how well a dyad works to mend a relationship. In his work, Dr John Gottman frequently discusses attempts at repair. All types of relationships, including those between parents and children, can be successfully handled using the same techniques. It is like a window—when it gets broken, repair is needed to keep it strong and functioning. Without repair, the window may remain in place, but it will not perform as intended. He contends that individuals in healthy relationships are capable of making and accepting attempts at mending quickly and frequently.

You may be surprised to know that repair attempts are demonstrated by babies, too. All of us are born with an innate tendency to repair breakdowns in connection with our loved ones. Even infants cheerfully contribute to repairs with their looks, smiles, motions, cries, and protests.

Are You Attuned to Each Other?

Attunement is an interaction rhythm in which partners exchange positive emotions. Researchers Ed Tronick and Andrew Gianino determined the frequency newborns and their caregivers are attuned to one another. They discovered it to be quite little. Only 30 per cent of the time do carers and babies communicate in sync, even in strong, trusting relationships. The remaining 70 per cent consist of incompatible, out-of-sync, or in the process of being fixed and put back together. In their study, they found that most of the time, carers and babies were in a state of 'dysregulated attunement'. This is where their interactions were out of sync or in the process of being restored to a positive rhythm. This suggests that even in the most ideal of circumstances, it can be difficult for carers and babies to stay attuned to each other and maintain positive emotions if one is not mindful of it.

Tronick says that these inconsistencies and fixes are significant. They are crucial for children's developing self-regulation, coping skills, and resilience. For instance, when an infant is distressed, their caregiver can calm them with a song, a hug, or by making silly faces. These small interventions help the child learn how to self-regulate, cope, and become resilient. Through these mismatches, babies and children learn that the world does not always meet their expectations as they grow. Through these small exposures to the micro-stress and distressing feelings followed by the happy feelings that precede repair, or coming back together, they gain valuable experience of keeping their boat afloat. In other words, if a carer fully addressed all of their child's demands, it would hinder the child's growth. This is akin to learning to ride a bike—if you never have a chance to practise on your own, you will never learn how to stay balanced and avoid crashing. On the other hand, if you are provided with a space to fall a few times and pick yourself back up, you can eventually learn how to stay upright.

According to UCLA neuropsychiatrist Dan Siegel, director of the Mindsight Centre and author of multiple books on interpersonal neurobiology, 'Repairing ruptures is the most critical thing in parenting.' According to Tronick, life is a sequence of mismatches, miscommunications, and misattunements that are swiftly fixed before becoming disorganised and stressful again, requiring them to be fixed once more. When a rupture occurs, parents must acknowledge it, validate their children's feelings, and work with them to repair it. This helps children develop a secure attachment to their parents, which allows them to better process, regulate, and express their emotions. This, in turn, can help them develop better communication skills and forge more successful relationships with others.

The degree to which the child is impacted depends on their ability to speak up during the argument. This depends on whether they get the chance to be open and honest about their feelings and find closure later. But even the tiniest disputes and misunderstandings might need to be resolved. This is like a house of cards—even the slightest breeze of conflict can cause it to come crashing down. Thus, it's crucial to address problems quickly and delicately to ensure that the foundations of love, openness, and flexibility remain intact.

There are various ways to forge a connection and express regret. When the intention is there, repair automatically takes place. Warm connection, making space for them, spending time doing what they enjoy, warm compassion, play, and humour can help to repair the connection. It doesn't always need to be discussed. Yet, many arguments send the child messages about who they are and how you see them. Children often experience feelings of defectiveness and self-hatred when they perceive rejection from their parents regarding their identities and preferences. Remember, they might not express these feelings verbally, instead they may display behavioural issues.

How to Make Repair Attempts?

Taking the time to give your child attention and listen to them when they need it shows them that you are attentive to their needs and care about their well-being. This can help heal a broken relationship between the two of you and nurture a strong connection. Mentioned below are some ways you can try at home as a parent or teenager to help you repair your relationship.

1. **Emotional Validation:** Conflict can be greatly reduced by letting the other person know that you understand them and value their feelings and experiences. Both

parents and adolescents frequently describe how they feel ignored and misunderstood by the other. One expresses 'I hear you' and 'I care about your feelings' by providing the other with some validation.

a. *For children:* Your parents could frequently feel invisible, taken for granted, and unimportant to you. It can reduce their rage, damaged sentiments, and potential defensiveness by validating their emotions. Keep in mind that your parents are also emotional beings.

b. *For parents:* How often have you heard children claim that nobody understands them? That may be partly because grown-ups don't always do a good job of recognising their feelings. For example, when a child comes home from school feeling sad or angry, a parent might try to cheer them up by saying 'Come on, don't be so sad; it's not that bad.' This can be invalidating to the child and make them feel misunderstood or unheard. Instead, you might show your child that you want to understand them and are there for them, no matter how they are feeling by validating their feelings.

2. **Be Accountable and Apologise:** De-escalating a situation can be accomplished, in large part, by accepting responsibility and expressing regret for your part in the event or conflict.

   a. *For children:* Typically, parents want their children to understand what they did wrong, accept responsibility for their decisions, and learn not to repeat the behaviour. The sooner the issue is resolved, the sooner you can take responsibility for your part.

b. *For parents:* Youngsters frequently think that parents won't own up to their mistakes or that they can make poor decisions, too. Hearing a parent express regret and accept responsibility for their errors can be motivating for children. In this way, parents also teach their children the value of this skill. For example, if a parent makes a mistake, such as being late to pick up their child from school, they can apologise and explain why they were late. They can also explain how they plan to ensure it doesn't happen again.

3. **'Stop Action' Strategies:** Before someone becomes overwhelmed or situations escalate, Gottman offers some excellent techniques to halt fighting. Children might learn to identify when they are feeling overwhelmed and request a break, but it is also crucial to lead by example and encourage these behaviours. It is important to understand that these aren't conflict-resolution techniques; rather, they provide everyone a chance to de-stress and return the topic at hand in a more composed state. Gottman (1999) gives the following examples:

    - 'Let's take a break.'
    - 'Let's agree to disagree.'
    - 'I'm feeling overwhelmed.'
    - 'Can we change the topic and come back to this later?'

4. **Understanding through Empathy:** Along with validation, considering the dispute from the other party's perspective might help in reaching a peaceful conclusion.
    a. *For children:* Despite occasional feelings of unjust, parents' rules, punishments, and boundaries typically stem from a desire to provide for their children. When teenagers attempt to put themselves in their parents' position and understand that imposing curfews are not set to provoke them but to ensure their safety, for instance, it can shift the dynamics of the disagreement. Children could express appreciation by acknowledging, 'I understand that you set a curfew because you love me and want to keep me safe. I'm grateful for that.'
    b. *For parents:* Children often feel misunderstood, making it challenging for parents to comprehend their decisions and motivations. However, taking a moment to reevaluate their actions and empathise with their children's position may lead to mutual understanding. Parents might realise the importance of peer connections to their child when discussing phone usage. They could convey understanding by saying, 'I know your friends are important to you, and your phone is a vital means of staying connected outside of school. I understand that limiting your usage makes you worry about missing out on important events.

Importance of Feedback

It is vital that feedback from all family members is permitted in a family system. The family system depends on a healthy loop of back-and-forth information on collectively how each family member can express themselves freely. Unfortunately, in most families, there is a lack of system on a democratic communication pattern between various family members. Healthy family systems need healthy communication, no matter how uncomfortable it is. Hence, many families miss out on the importance of this vital lifestyle communication pattern.

Work through this Exercise

Do you minimise the hurts that children share with you?

Do you think it is okay to scold them for their own good only?

Do you tend to take out your own frustration about something else on them?

Do you deny your child's perception about something?

Do you realise that not validating your child's version of their reality can be akin to 'gaslighting'?

Answer Key

If you have answered 'yes' to even one of these, reading this book will be especially helpful for you to forge a supportive, deeper, and more meaningful connection with your child.

If your answer is an emphatic 'no', perhaps you are unwilling to explore the nature of your relationship with your own child, and you may be in denial. Digging deeper may help prevent many potential issues from arising in the future.

Children are far less intimidated by conflicts with others in general when domestic disputes are resolved. These abilities minimise emotions of helplessness, fear, and defensiveness when conflicts emerge, generally because the child has been enabled to be an active participant in resolving them at home. Children are typically much better at taking responsibility for their words and actions that negatively impact others, as well as being much better able to assert and hold boundaries when they have healthy conflict resolution modelled frequently in the family.

Effective conflict resolution techniques can help children grow into teenagers and eventually into adults who are less defensive, more forthright, more authentic, and willing to own up to their mistakes. When children are taught conflict resolution techniques, they remain calm and polite through challenging encounters, are not afraid to speak up for themselves or others when they need to, and are more likely to develop into peacemakers.

20

Healthy Strategies for Connecting with Your Teen

'Adolescents are not monsters. They are just people trying to learn how to make it among the adults in the world, who are probably not so sure themselves.'

—Virginia Satir

The relationship between parents and their teenagers is one of the most significant connections in a young individual's life. This connection is important because it influences the mental, emotional, and physical well-being of adolescents. Therefore, it is crucial for parents to invest time and effort in building strong, supportive relationships with their teenagers.

A strong connection between a parent and their teenager can positively impact the teenager's mental health. For instance, a study conducted in 2014 found that individuals with low self-esteem during adolescence exhibited more depressive symptoms two decades later in adulthood. Additionally, Jun et al. (2013) demonstrated that improving self-esteem in early adolescence can help prevent depression. Adolescence is a period of significant changes and challenges, and having an emotionally available and supportive parent can help teenagers navigate this difficult phase. Parents who maintain a strong connection with their teenagers can recognise signs of distress and provide the necessary emotional support to help them cope with stress and anxiety.

Furthermore, a strong parent-teen connection can positively influence the emotional development of a teenager. Teenagers who have a healthy relationship with their parents are more likely to possess higher self-esteem, a better sense of self-identity, and a positive outlook on life. This is akin to nurturing a plant with care and love; it will grow into a healthy and vibrant flower rather than one that is neglected and withers in an unforgiving environment. This is because parents who are strongly connected with their teenagers can provide a sense of security and stability essential for emotional development.

Healthy interactions between parents and adolescents can impact teenagers' physical health. Studies have shown that teenagers who have positive relationships with their parents are less likely to engage in risky behaviours such as drug use, sexual activity, and delinquent behaviour. This is because parents who are in tune with their teenagers can provide guidance and set clear boundaries, which help teenagers make healthy choices.

Teenagers frequently test boundaries, try new things, and experiment with independence as they grow up. They often turn to their parents, caretakers, or role models for a combination of support, direction, structure, and punishment. It's akin to a tightrope walker at a circus, trying to find the right balance between holding onto a safety line and pushing forward. Without the security of the safety line, the walker may feel lost and overwhelmed, but it's only by letting go and experimenting that they can truly find their footing. To demonstrate to young people that you are someone they can turn to with questions or concerns, exemplify trust, respect, honesty, and transparency.

Strengthening Connection with Teenagers

The connection between parents and their teenagers is essential for the well-being of the adolescents. Connections with a strong foundation can positively influence their mental, emotional, and physical health. Therefore, it is crucial that parents prioritise building and maintaining a healthy relationship with their teenagers to support their growth and development. Listed below are some tools that might help parents strengthen the bond:

1. **Paying Attention:** Being attentive, inquisitive, and open might help parents pick up on subtle remarks and information that reflect a young person's unique style of communication. Teenagers sometimes find it difficult to answer direct questions. When they don't feel pressured to disclose information they aren't comfortable sharing, young people may be more willing to open up to their parents.
2. **Validating their Feelings:** When adolescents' worries are taken seriously, they feel more empowered. This sense of empowerment promotes positive mental health and well-being, which can yield both short-term and long-term benefits. It's natural to want to find a solution as soon as a teenager shares a problem they're facing. However, it's also important to take the time to inquire about their emotions. Being present and offering a non-judgmental environment for them to articulate their struggles are effective ways to demonstrate empathy.
3. **Building Trust:** Parents can explore various methods to demonstrate trust in their teenagers. This could involve giving them specific tasks, soliciting their assistance, genuinely considering their input when

making decisions, and more. These actions show that parents have faith in their ability to help with important matters.

4. **Being Rationale:** Establishing norms and boundaries is crucial for parents or caregivers, but it may encounter opposition. Teens might be more receptive to decisions if parents explain the rationale behind them. It's okay for them to disagree with some decisions; parents can show trust and appreciation for their input into the relationship by providing context.
5. **Spending Time Together:** There are numerous ways to connect and spend quality time with children. Engaging in activities both parties enjoy—such as cooking, watching a movie, sharing meals, taking a walk or drive, etc.—without discussing personal matters can strengthen the bond and pave the way for more challenging conversations. It's important for children to have opportunities to bond with their parents and share enjoyable experiences.
6. **Giving Compliments:** Many teenagers value support from others and care about what their parents or caregivers think of them. Look for opportunities, no matter how small, to offer encouragement and support. This can be expressed in several ways, such as sating 'Thanks for walking the dog,' 'I love your outfit today,' 'I can see that you're a great friend,' etc.

Ways to Deal with Failure

Failure and shortcomings are necessary parts of being human. Failure comes to all of us in many ways, big and small, and it also happens to children. When they experience these mistakes, whether parents use process-praise or person-praise, it has a significant impact on their mindset. By repeatedly telling them things like, 'You are very good at Maths, good job!' parents can encourage their children to have a fixed mindset, leading them to attribute failure to a lack of effort or dedication rather than their inherent abilities.

Person-praise fails to instil in children the idea that they can improve their mathematical abilities through hard work and devotion. Children who receive constant compliments about themselves lose motivation when they fail because they have misconceptions about why they failed. If they understand that personal attributes play a role in both success and failure, they will have more control over the situation. Children are less likely to exert effort in class or in areas where they struggle if praised individually. Such praise weakens self-control. Some may declare, 'Maths is just not for me,' or 'My brain just doesn't work that way,' instead of realising they need to devote more time and effort to the subject. Failure, like success, is falsely believed to be determined by personal traits, rather than effort.

Children are taught through person-praise that failure is due to a lack of some quality or trait. In reality, it's a result of a lack of ability, commitment, or poor problem-solving skills. Problem-solving ability, skill, and determination are all adaptable qualities that can be improved! Children are taught via process-praise that failure is a result of what they did or did not do, giving them the opportunity to change their strategy. Children learn that they can learn from failures and mistakes when we use process-praise. They discover the power to grow and learn from these failures. Instead of serving as a pretext for harsh personal judgment, failure becomes an opportunity for personal development.

When children think, 'I did it once, but I'm not sure if I can do it again,' compliments might make them feel anxious. When these compliments involve comparisons, they can also induce stress. Saying, 'You accomplished more than she did!' implies a competition where your child might feel they could lose at any moment. Besides, some children become stunned when receiving accolades because they lack the words to respond. They may either argue by saying, 'That's not true!' or criticise themselves with, 'I did a lousy job!' to avoid appearing arrogant. Thus, if parents believe their child may downplay praise or see it with mistrust or suspicion, they can work with them to address these issues.

Praise as a Routine Affair

Parents can teach their children that being modest simply means not feeling superior to anyone, regardless of their accomplishments or traits. Additionally, when parents start speaking in a kind and pleasant manner at home, it makes praise a routine occurrence. A tool that benefits children for the rest of their life is encouraging them to grow up appreciating themselves and feeling worthwhile. Understanding how to accept praise, nevertheless, does not imply relying on them.

Why do Teenagers Reject Praise?

Most adolescents are happy to receive a genuine compliment. However, there are occasions when compliments make them cringe or feel embarrassed. When praised, some teenagers may lash out in rage, argue, or cover their ears (Kennedy-Moore, 'When Your Child Hates Compliments'). Here are a few explanations for why some children find getting compliments to be so unsettling:

a. For starters, children with social anxiety often think that people constantly stare at them and pass judgement. When someone compliments them, they feel that everyone is watching them, deciding whether they deserve the praise in the first place.

b. Furthermore, it can intensify negative self-focus and self-judgment when a compliment does not match what youngsters perceive about themselves. Overstated praise such as 'You're fantastic!' can backfire by getting teenagers to concentrate on all the ways they are not 'amazing'.

How to Communicate Appreciation?

With these suggestions, parents can effectively communicate their appreciation. Expressing what they appreciate is important. When parents are proud of an action, however small, expressing it is important. Over time, the little things parents say to their child might accumulate to have a significant impact on them.

a) Seek non-verbal cues to praise or inspire your child. Parents giving their child a thumbs-up, a smile, or a high five can be effective methods to express their admiration for their actions or efforts.

b) As a surprise for their exemplary behaviour, parents might treat their child. For instance, 'Thanks for picking up the toys. Let's celebrate in the park!'

c) Watch for small successes and adjustments. Praise any attempt or development rather than waiting until your child has completed something flawlessly.

d) Strive to provide more compliments than criticism. As

a general rule, aim to compliment your child five times every time you criticise them.

e) Parents might encourage youngsters to be enthusiastic about their own interests and compliment them on their strengths. This will help the child gain pride and self-confidence as a result.

f) Research suggests that parents should make an effort to match their praise for their child's desirable behaviour. The child might not accept the parent's praise if it is overstated.

g) Use age-appropriate methods for rewarding good behaviour. For instance, although toddlers might like being singled out for praise, teenagers might not want to be publicly applauded for their accomplishments.

In parenting, appreciation and more appreciation is key. When teens feel appreciated, they are less reactive and more willing to listen to different points of views, including yours, dear parent. If you have often wondered why your connection with your teenager is raspy, it is time to voice the obvious—your appreciation. These realisations, simple suggestions, and strategies ensure that parenting efforts to connect remain healthy and yield positive results.

21

Love: The Ultimate Force

'My love for you is like an invisible elastic band. No matter how far you go, we are connected.'
—Anonymous

A cat never ignores a mewling kitten. Yet, human beings constantly ask their children for 'explanations' when the children share their concerns. It is not uncommon to hear parents complaining to their children about how the child is slowing them down or hindering something or the other. Do you think after hearing so much about how they are a hindrance or ways they could be better, they have the foundation for healthy relationships with others as well as their own selves? Healthy intrapersonal relationships provide a strong base of self-confidence and of healthy self-esteem. Children learn self-esteem before the age of five when they see unconditional love and approval in their parents' eyes. Thus, do you think constantly checking on them helps their self-esteem? No one is denying the parents' good intentions; however, the road to hell is paved with good intentions.

We are very conditional when our children show certain emotions like disgust or anger. Many parenting books recommend a 'time-out' when a child acts up. In effect what they mean is, ignore a two-year-old who is throwing a tantrum.

But dismissing a child's anger or reprimanding them for it or excluding them for expressing it creates a void in the child. The child grows up learning to disown parts of their own self. Furthermore, they learn to hide their feelings with the parents as well as others. Over time, these repressed feelings create anxiety, restlessness, resentment, along with breakdowns in communication.

By the time a child grows into an adolescent, they may have lost all respect for their own self, which also reflects in their attitude and disrespect towards the parents.

What Works in Therapy?

In my experience as a therapist, most adolescents misbehave because they feel rejected, misunderstood, discounted, and dismissed by their parents for who they are and how they want to live their lives. Ultimately, what works for them in therapy is the simple realisation that 'I am good enough,' 'I am worthy of love,' and 'I am capable.' As their self-confidence grows, they become interested in knowing what works for them in the moment, using those resources to build themselves up instead of being on a self-sabotaging spree or going on a battle of wills with their parents. My book *Emotional Ability Resources* has proved to be helpful for many in this journey.

However, if you are a parent, do not despair. The beauty of the human spirit is in its flexibility and openness to change.

Setting Healthy Boundaries with Love

Boundaries is one area where there tends to be conflict between parents and teens. Curfews, type of groups, peers, interests, priorities, diets, choices in terms of clothes, food, dating, pocket money, lifestyle, social life, sports, academics the list is endless. Canadian physician Gabor Maté says that it is possible to set healthy boundaries with warmth and love.

When a child is loved without conditions and encouraged to explore and develop their independence, play in nature, and be curious about new things, they grow up in an atmosphere of unconditional support and acceptance.

By the time they reach their teenage years, children are often willing to look up to their parents for support and even follow their advice. If we observe mammals in nature, such as gorillas, we see nurturing behaviours. A gorilla hugs its infant close to its body, providing safety, warmth, and nurturing. In times of imminent danger from other predators, the gorilla doesn't reprimand its offspring for causing difficulty or stress, or for slowing them down in their attempt to escape. Instead, they swiftly gather their young and flee, moving as quickly as possible given the circumstances. There's no disapproval or reprimanding their children.

Love Languages for Teenagers

Dr Gary Chapman's book, *The 5 Love Languages: The Secret to Love That Lasts*, has been a bestseller for decades and has helped countless people understand and communicate their love for others in a way that is meaningful and effective. The five love languages that Chapman identifies are:

- Words of affirmation
- Acts of service
- Receiving gifts
- Quality time
- Physical touch

(The five love languages are mentioned in detail in Chapter 6.)

Each person has a primary love language that speaks to them most strongly, and understanding this can help improve relationships with those around us.

For teenagers, understanding and utilising these love languages can be especially important. Adolescence is a time of great emotional and social change, and being able to effectively communicate love and affection can make a huge difference in how teenagers feel about themselves. Socially, mentally, and spiritually, teenagers face a variety of anxieties every day. The trick is to understand your teenager's love language and try to communicate with them in their language of choice. You can take the quiz on 5lovelanguages.com to understand your own and your teenager's love language.

Unconditional Love

Unconditional love is the guiding light that shines in the darkness and helps parents know where they are and what they need to do to raise their children. Without this kind of love, parenting is a mess. The best way to define unconditional love is by demonstrating its actions. Parents love their children regardless of their looks, assets, liabilities, disabilities, expectations, and behaviour. However, this does not mean parents like everything their children do. It simply means that they always tell their children when they behave poorly. It means giving and showing love.

In conclusion, understanding and utilising the five love languages can be a powerful tool for teenagers as they navigate the emotional and social challenges of adolescence. By understanding their own love language and those of their loved ones, they can communicate love and affection in a way that is meaningful and effective.

The Role of Vulnerability in Healthy Relationships with Adolescents

Ten years ago, there wasn't much talk about emotional vulnerability. Being emotionally vulnerable has generally been compared to being weak or at least slightly hurt or frightened. Perhaps it's a natural, routine, and unavoidable part of our existence as humans, and it's not discussed much because it feels scary.

Emotional vulnerability is most commonly felt as a fear of being rejected, humiliated, or judged inappropriately. Brené Brown defines this as 'uncertainty, risk, and emotional exposure.' Uncertainty accompanies us every day and is closely related to fear. In fact, people who suffer from chronic anxiety often find it particularly difficult to accept uncertainty in their daily lives. For example, the risk of feeling rejected when your love isn't reciprocated. These situations can be more frightening for some than others, depending on our personal histories, cultural backgrounds, and basic personality traits. It poses certain risks to many people. However, most people struggle with some degree of emotional vulnerability every day.

Letting your children into your life requires being vulnerable with them. It's safer for your children to reveal themselves to you if you open up more to them. When you share your fears with them, they will share their own. They will turn to you when things get difficult if they know you share their sentiments. Since you've been there, they can relate to you without passing judgment. Their trust will be built on the foundation of your genuineness. Being vulnerable makes it easier for us to accept criticism and realise that each of us has a part to play in helping the other person become their best self.

Accountability encompasses more than just creating a set of guidelines and penalties. It entails carrying out our obligation to elevate one another as human beings. Adolescents will be able to do the same with you if they know they can call you out for not walking the walk. Real and pertinent conversations will occur at such times. Each of us has a responsibility to the other (Angela Karanja 2020).

Adolescents, as humans, are inspired by parents' willingness to expose their true selves, share their errors, and express their feelings in this vulnerable way. In fact, research demonstrates that parents are more trusted when they express their vulnerability, resulting in a closer bond with their teenagers. Many parents of adolescent children desire to be viewed favourably by their children. Unfortunately, most of them go to great lengths to show how fantastic they are and how they have never done anything wrong or failed at anything in an effort to present themselves in the best possible light. Even when it is obvious that something is wrong, they stand stoic, ignore it, and act as though they are not in agony, as though nothing is wrong in their world. They essentially present themselves as flawless.

While the media and society may encourage this, when parents of teenagers act in this way, they are sending a powerful but damaging message to their teenagers, the message that they are perfect and being vulnerable is shameful. When teenagers see their parents as having it all together and figured out, it can make them feel like a burden because they believe that the same level of perfection is required of them. Unfortunately, this causes people to believe they will never be able to reach this degree of perfection, which destroys their self-esteem. Teenagers, though, may see all the grandeur, which is excellent. However, parents do their children an injustice if they aren't open enough to reveal the specifics of the tale behind the glory.

Sometimes, it is not intentional. As Robert Jackman writes in *Healing Your Lost Inner Child: How to Stop Impulsive Reactions, Set Healthy Boundaries, and Embrace Authentic Life* that parents are often unwilling to dig deeper into their own emotional wounding and have 'emotional amnesia.' He adds, 'We develop this emotional amnesia to some of our harshest realities because we instinctively know the deep pain that lies below the surface. As we heal, our minds open up space for old memories to surface.' When we heal, we are willing to be authentic and become emotionally available as well.

Emotional Availability

Parents who are emotionally available ensure that they are aware of facet of their child's life, including school. They are ready to put in effort into helping their child learn rather than expecting the school to 'raise' their child. This simply means that they are available for their child's general well-being. It does not imply that they adopt a helicopter parenting style or demand flawless academic achievement from their child.

Emotional availability in parent-child relationships predicts a wide range of child outcomes. First, emotional availability significantly relates to child attachment security, both with parents and professional caregivers (Altenhofen et al. 2013). Studies have shown that emotional management in children is also connected to emotional availability, particularly, in a sample of low-income mother-child pairs. Children who had more emotional insight in their connection showed better emotional regulation in trying circumstances (Little and Carter 2005). In fact, interestingly, contrary to popular perception, children who are severely inhibited or perceived as socially awkward tend to have better control of their stress responses.

While it is crucial for parents to devote time and effort to their children, it is important not to overdo things and make them entitled. No amount of material things or classes can substitute emotional connection or meaningful interactions; parents need to remember this simple, cardinal truth. Overcompensating for time away from children due to other priorities and commitments is disastrous in hindsight. Engaging in dialogue and clear communication, rather than resorting to appeasement, is a beneficial approach that fosters closeness and mutual satisfaction.

Statements such as 'My demands need to be met as soon as I voice them,' 'Right now, come what may,' or 'I don't care how you do it but I need it now,' serve as precursors to development of entitlement rather than genuine love. This entitlement mindset, characterised by 'everything better go my way' or 'it has to happen the moment I ask for it,' diminishes empathy, reduces the capacity to tolerate discomfort, and fosters a self-centred, selfish adult mindset. Consequently, it often leads to challenges in interpersonal relationships.

Healthy Parenting

Healthy parenting involves fine-tuning expectations with clear explanations and lots of emotional support. Investing ample time to nurture clear thinking and mutual growth mindset rather than appeasing them with instant indulgence is crucial. Be mindful of the impact of sowing control patterns and power dynamic entitlements or struggles in a growing mind. Substituting material wants with a lack of time and nurturing towards mutual growth lays the foundational stone for personality disorders like narcissism to develop later in life. Therefore, it is important to keep maintain equilibrium.

When parents are emotionally available to their teenagers while still allowing them the room to develop into adults, children thrive. Even when feeling overburdened by daily obligations, emotional presence is possible once a parent is aware and conscious about providing it. The best part is that it is free and as widely available as you, the parent, want to avail of it.

Parents can take comfort in the fact that the greatest value their parenting can offer is being emotionally present to their children. A strong parent-child relationship requires both parties to be emotionally vibrant, accessible, and present. After all, parents are in the driver's seat, so the onus to set the tone of interaction lies with parents and not on what children are doing 'wrong' or how they are 'acting out'. Understanding and realigning the 'why' behind troublesome actions is the best way to change the dynamics of parent-adolescent interactions. This compassionate and responsible approach creates a climate of love and support for growing teens and sets them up for future happiness and success, too.

Refer to the table (on page 226) on how attachment styles, boundaries, vulnerability, how we handle rejection, building trust, and emotional intimacy are all interlinked.

Strategies to Create Warmth

Would you like your children to warm up to you? If the answer is a resounding 'yes', please read on.

There is a list of specific strategies that you can consciously adopt to create warmth and make yourself more attractive to your teens. Before you dismiss this idea as strange, I urge you to pause and consider. Think for a moment about a social gathering or an important family function you have to

Attachment Style	Boundaries	Vulnerability	Processing of Rejection	Trust	Emotional Intimacy
Secure	Able to establish and enforce boundaries with others	Maintains stability and feels secure in a relationship	Able to handle and control feelings of disappointment and rejection	Having an easy time placing faith in others	Capable of communicating and being comfortable with emotional intimacy
Avoidant	Constraints due to the sensation of being choked or entangled; one may be inflexible or flexible	Tends to be fiercely independent and wary of letting people in	Shutting down or withdrawing when they feel overwhelmed, rejected, or triggered	Difficult to trust others and feel independent	Withdrawing and establishing more distance in the relationship as a coping mechanism
Anxious	Having trouble setting boundaries, sharing excessively, or feeling anxious and abandoned when someone doesn't reciprocate	Expressing their wants discreetly, often in a passive-aggressive manner	Persistent concern of being abandoned or rejected	Always seeking assurances that the relationship is going smoothly	Profound emotional sensitivity yet lack of self-advocacy
Disorganised	Initiating arguments or abruptly removing significant others from their lives in an effort to cope	Relationship difficulties stem from profound sentiments of worthlessness and security concerns	Possessing irrational expectations for relationships and experiencing being betrayed or rejected when an issue emerges	Fluctuates between unpredictable and inconsistent patterns across anxious and avoidant behaviour	Reluctant to share too much of themselves as a means of safeguarding themselves from potential harm; keep their partner at a distance to avoid emotions

attend. Regardless of whether you feel happy, bored, or slightly irritated, you typically put in an effort to clean up and present yourself well. At the event, you try to mingle and are generally open to warming up to at least a few people. As adults, most of us either avoid gatherings or choose to be somewhat affable, at the very least. But when it comes to interacting with our own children, we often don't pause to think about how desirable our tone is and whether we're consciously setting the tone for them to warm up to us.

Here is a checklist of some helpful strategies to encourage them to warm up and be receptive towards spending time with you:

- Be open-minded
- Maintain a positive attitude
- Smile often
- Display relaxed body language
- Keep your tone calm and soothing
- Avoid yelling as a general rule
- Apologise if you have overstepped
- Maintain healthy boundaries
- Refrain from snooping through their cupboards or phones
- Be honest
- Keep their secrets when they confide in you
- Remain consistent
- Refrain from justifying your irritation
- Avoid giving confusing signals
- Refrain from criticising
- Do not preach
- Trust them
- Keep their trust

- Appreciate them
- Avoid blaming

Live life as if it were a celebration, not a drudgery to be endured. Remember, it's not your child's fault if you're having a hard day or going through a difficult life experience. There may be circumstances that provoke you or make you want to reprimand them or make them see sense. But pause and ask yourself, 'Will any of the reactions bubbling inside me be helpful in inspiring them to change? What would truly facilitate the possibility of fulfilling my expectations from my teenager? A climate of warmth or one filled with tension and strife?'

Are you ready to take a smarter parenting approach and use one, if not multiple, of the strategies mentioned above—as well as any others you find useful—to create a climate of warmth? Just this pause in thinking and self-reflection sets the stage for multiple choices instead of a rapid-fire barrage of words uttered in the heat of the moment.

In any given situation, you can make a healthy choice as a parent. A gentle, conscious reminder to appreciate the simple fact that 'I am experiencing parenthood, courtesy of X, Y, Z,' creates warmth within you and usually does the trick.

In fine, what ultimately matters is how we understand and use these concepts to relate to teenagers in a loving, accepting, and authentic manner. Healthy relationships embrace vulnerability and are open to balancing relationships by respecting boundaries. Children thrive when parents are emotionally mature and aware of realities, willing to adapt to them instead of resisting them. As parents channel more love and appreciation into their parenting, relationships transform into constructive interactions, leading to a healthy environment for everyone.

Afterword

Reconnecting with your teens is possible. All one needs is an intention to form a link with them. Therefore, I congratulate you for embarking on this journey, as simply by picking up a copy of this book, your intention is clear.

Reading this book is the next step in the right direction. It shows your determination to do whatever it takes to spark a connection with your teenager and understand how to strengthen and rekindle your bond with each other.

Parenting is a lifelong journey that requires patience and curiosity. For their welfare and benefit, become curious about their thinking. Ask them questions and listen to them even when you do not agree with them. Consider their perspective. Would you be the same if you were a teenager today?

This approach helps you move from fear of what could go wrong to a place of trust and fearlessness where you know you have raised them well to climb any mountains they choose to scale. Worry and anxiety about their well-being reduce drastically when you honestly look at yourself and realise that you have transformed from that gawky teenager to the individual you are today.

In a nutshell, convey your confidence in their ability to be successful and balanced as adults. Be courageous and let them learn from their mistakes. Not everything your parents told you worked for you; understand that it's the same for them.

If you have the desire to connect, it is important to prioritise that connection. Loving relationships aren't created by being busy, worrying about your child's future, or lamenting about how stressed you are about your own issues. Spending time together, being willing to introspect and understand your unfulfilled desires, and sharing your own journey is the right way to move forward. Do not expect to magically create a healthy relationship. If needed, seek help from a licensed mental health practitioner.

Between desire and action lies this chasm of actual time devoted to building this important relationship. I wish you the best.

Happy Parenting!

Acknowledgements

I am deeply grateful to the patients, students, and counselees who have entrusted me with their stories and vulnerabilities. Your courage and resilience continually i nspire me, reminding me of the boundless strength of the human spirit.

I express my sincere appreciation to my mentors for generously sharing their expertise, unwavering support, and boundless motivation throughout this journey.

My heartfelt gratitude goes out to my family, whose love and solidarity have been a constant source of strength. Special thanks to Jyoti, Stuti, and Aryana for their warmth and unwavering support.

I am profoundly grateful to my husband, Mr. Sumit Sureka, whose understanding, love, contributions, and active support have been the cornerstone of this endeavour. Without his encouragement, this book would not have come to fruition.

Lastly, my deepest thanks to my children, Abhyuday and Nandini, for their love and steadfast belief in me. Your unwavering faith has been my greatest inspiration.

Bibliography

'From Esther Perel's Blog - Rituals for Healthy Relationships at Every Stage.' Esther Perel's Blog. Accessed February 20, 2024. https://www.estherperel.com/blog/rituals-for-healthy-relationships.

'Parent-Child Relationship and Its Effect on Adolescents: Free Essay Example.' *StudyCorgi*. Accessed February 20, 2024. https://studycorgi.com/parent-child-relationship-and-its-effect-on-adolescents/.

'Rituals Strengthen Couples. Here's Why They're Good for Business, Too.' *HBS Working Knowledge*, June 27, 2019. https://hbswk.hbs.edu/item/rituals-strengthen-couples-here-s-why-they-re-good-for-business-too.

'Teenage Parenting: Problems of Children and Parent: Free Essay Example.' *StudyCorgi*. Accessed February 20, 2024. https://studycorgi.com/teenage-parenting-problems-of-children-and-parent/.

Aggarwal, Parul. 'A Study of Stress among Adolescent Students in Relation to Their Emotional Maturity and Family Climate.' *International Journal of Research in Social Sciences* 8, no. 4 (2018): 106-117.

Allen, James R., and Barbara Ann Allen. 'Scripts: The Role of Permission.' *Transactional Analysis Bulletin* 2, no. 2 (1972): 72–74. DOI: 10.1177/036215377200200021.

Alonso-Stuyck, Paloma. 'Parenting and Healthy Teenage Lifestyles.' *International Journal of Environmental Research and Public Health* 17, no. 15 (2020): 5428. 10.3390/ijerph17155428. DOI: 10.3390/ijerph17155428.

--------------. 'Which Parenting Style Encourages Healthy Lifestyles in Teenage Children? Proposal for a Model of Integrative Parenting Styles.' *International Journal of Environmental Research and Public Health* 16, no. 11 (2019): 2057. DOI: 10.3390/ijerph16112057.

Altenhofen, Shannon, Robert Clyman, Carrie Little, Maria Baker, and Zeynep Biringen. 'Attachment security in three-year-olds who entered substitute care in infancy.' *Infant Mental Health Journal* 34 (2013): 435–445. DOI: 10.1002/imhj.21401.

Armstrong, Mary I., and Roger A. Boothroyd. 'Predictors of Emotional Well-being in At-risk Adolescent Girls: Developing Preventive Intervention Strategies.' *The Journal of Behavioral Health Services & Research* 35, no. 4 (2008): 435–453. DOI: 10.1007/s11414-006-9048-9.

Arnett, Jeffrey Jensen. 'Emerging Adulthood: A Theory of Development from the Late Teens through the Twenties.' *American Psychologist* 55, no. 5 (2000): 469. DOI: 10.1037/0003-066X.55.5.469.

Arnett, Jeffrey Jensen. 'Learning to Stand Alone: The Contemporary American Transition to Adulthood in Cultural and Historical Context.' *Human Development* 41, no. 5-6 (1998): 295–315. DOI: 10.1159/000022591.

Aslan, Sevda, and Selahattin Gelbal. 'Separation-individuation of late adolescents: A longitudinal study.' *Educational Research and Reviews* 11, no. 1 (2016): 1–15. DOI: 10.5897/ERR2015.2570.

Baker, Charlene K., Fran H. Norris, Eric C. Jones, and Arthur D. Murphy. 'Childhood Trauma and Adulthood Physical Health in Mexico.' *Journal of Behavioral Medicine* 32 (2009): 255–269. DOI: 10.1007/s10865-009-9199-2.

Brindle, Ryan C., Matthew R. Cribbet, Laura B. Samuelsson, Chenlu Gao, Ellen Frank, Robert T. Krafty, Julian F. Thayer, Daniel J. Buysse, and Martica H. Hall. 'The Relationship between Childhood Trauma and Poor Sleep Health in Adulthood.' *Psychosomatic Medicine* 80, no. 2 (2018): 200. DOI: 10.1097/PSY.0000000000000542.

Brody, Gene H., Tianyi Yu, Steven RH Beach, Steven M. Kogan, Michael Windle, and Robert A. Philibert. 'Harsh Parenting and Adolescent Health: A Longitudinal Analysis with Genetic Moderation.' *Health Psychology* 33, no. 5 (2014): 401. DOI: 10.1037/a0032686.

Brouard, M., and G. Johnston. 'Romance Chimique ou la Question de la Séparation: Consommation d'Ecstasy à l'Adolescence.' *Neuropsychiatrie de l'Enfance et de l'Adolescence* 57, no. 5 (2009): 372–378.

Bulanda, Ronald E., and Debarun Majumdar. 'Perceived Parent–Child Relations and Adolescent Self-esteem.' *Journal of Child and Family Studies* 18 (2009): 203–212.

Coates, Dominiek. 'Impact of Childhood Abuse: Biopsychosocial Pathways through Which Adult Mental Health Is Compromised.' *Australian Social Work* 63, no. 4 (2010): 391-403. DOI: 10.1080/0312407X.2010.508533.

Crocetti, Elisabetta, Susan Branje, Monica Rubini, Hans M. Koot, and Wim Meeus. 'Identity Processes and Parent–Child and Sibling Relationships in Adolescence: A Five-wave Multi-informant Longitudinal Study.' *Child Development* 88, no. 1 (2017): 210-228. DOI: 10.1111/cdev.12547.

DeVore, Elise R., and Kenneth R. Ginsburg. 'The Protective Effects of Good Parenting on Adolescents.' *Current Opinion in Pediatrics* 17, no. 4 (2005): 460–465. DOI: 10.1097/01.mop.0000170514.27649.c9.

Draghici, Alexander. '10 Signs and Examples of Emotional Maturity.' *Happier Human*, February 15, 2023. https://www.happierhuman.com/emotional-maturity/.

Erskine, Richard G. 'Life Scripts: Unconscious Relational Patterns and Psychotherapeutic Involvement.' *Relational Patterns, Therapeutic Presence: Concepts and Practice of Integrative Psychotherapy*, 1-28. Routledge, 2018. DOI: 10.4324/9780429479519-6.

Erskine, Richard G., and Rebecca L. Trautmann. 'Methods of an Integrative Psychotherapy.' *Transactional Analysis Journal* 26, no. 4 (1996): 316–328. DOI: 10.1177/036215379602600410.

Fiese, Barbara H. 'Dimensions of Family Rituals across Two Generations: Relation to Adolescent Identity. *Family Process* 31, no. 2 (1992): 151–162. DOI: 10.1111/j.1545-5300.1992.00151.x.

Fiese, Barbara H., and Christine A. Kline. 'Development of the Family Ritual Questionnaire: Initial Reliability and Validation Studies.' *Journal of Family Psychology* 6, no. 3 (1993): 290. DOI: 10.1037/0893-3200.6.3.290.

Fosshage, James L. 'The Explicit and Implicit Domains in Psychoanalytic Change.' *Psychoanalytic Inquiry* 25, no. 4 (2005): 516–539. DOI: 0.2513/s07351690pi2504_7.

García, Fernando, and Enrique Gracia. 'The Indulgent Parenting Style and Developmental Outcomes in South European and Latin American Countries.' In *Parenting across Cultures: Childrearing, Motherhood and Fatherhood in Non-Western Cultures*, 419–433. DOI: 10.1007/978-94-007-7503-9_31.

Gold, Jerry, and George Stricker. 'Integrative Approaches to Psychotherapy.' In *Essential Psychotherapies: Theory and Practice*, 443–480.

Goulding, Mary McClure, and Robert L. Goulding. *Changing Lives through Redecision Therapy*. Grove Press, 1997.

Heaven, Patrick C. L. *The Social Psychology of Adolescence*. Basingstoke: Palgrave, 2001.

Hogue, Aaron, Molly Bobek, and Alexandra MacLean. 'Core Elements of CBT for Adolescent Conduct and Substance Use Problems: Comorbidity, Clinical Techniques, and Case Examples.' *Cognitive and Behavioral Practice* 27, no. 4 (2020): 426–441. DOI: 10.1016/j.cbpra.2019.12.002.

Houston, Elaine, B.Sc. 'CBT for Children: A Guide for Helping Kids in Therapy.' *PositivePsychology.com*, September 20, 2023. https://positivepsychology.com/cbt-for-children/.

Johnson, Zachary V., and Larry J. Young. 'Neurobiological Mechanisms of Social Attachment and Pair Bonding.' *Current Opinion in Behavioral Sciences* 3 (2015): 38–44. DOI: 10.1016/j.cobeha.2015.01.009.

Karanja, Angela. 'How Being Vulnerable As A Parent Benefits Your Relationship With Your Teen.' *Child Psychology*, October 28, 2020. https://www.raisingremarkableteenagers.com/post/how-being-vulnerable-as-a-parent-benefits-your-teen.

Kennedy-Moore, Eileen, Ph.D. 'When Your Child Hates Compliments: Praise Makes Some Children Uncomfortable. Here's How to Help.' Psychology Today, December 31, 2019. Accessed March 6, 2024. https://www.psychologytoday.com/us/blog/growing-friendships/201912/when-your-child-hates-compliments.

Lamborn, Susie D., and Dang-Giao T. Nguyen. 'African American Adolescents' Perceptions of Family Interactions: Kinship Support, Parent–Child Relationships, and Teen Adjustment.' *Journal of Youth and Adolescence* 33 (2004): 547–558. DOI: 10.1023/B:JOYO.0000048068.55441.d6.

Lamothe, Cindy. 'Are You Emotionally Mature?' *Healthline*, March 30, 2020. https://www.healthline.com/health/mental-health/emotional-maturity.

Lee, Sang Min, M. Harry Daniels, and Daniel B. Kissinger. 'Parental Influences on Adolescent Adjustment: Parenting Styles versus Parenting Practices.' *The Family Journal* 14, no. 3 (2006): 253–259. DOI: 10.1177/1066480706287.

Lindberg, Sara. 'Be the Best Parent You Can Be: Building Your Parenting Skills.' *Healthline*, September 28, 2020. https://www.healthline.com/health/parenting/parenting-skills.

Linley, P. Alex, Stephen Joseph, Susan Harrington, and Alex M. Wood. 'Positive Psychology: Past, Present, and (Possible) Future.' *The Journal of Positive Psychology* 1, no. 1 (2006): 3–16. DOI: 10.1080/17439760500372796.

Little, Carrie, and Alice Carter. 'Negative emotional reactivity and regulation in 12-month-olds following emotional challenge: contributions of maternal-infant emotional availability in a low-income sample.' *Infant Mental Health Journal* 26 (2005): 354–368. doi:10.1002/imhj.20055.

Lochman, John E., Nicole P. Powell, Caroline L. Boxmeyer, and Luis Jimenez-Camargo. 'Cognitive-Behavioral Therapy for Externalizing Disorders in Children and Adolescents.' *Child and Adolescent Psychiatric Clinics* 20, no. 2 (2011): 305–318. DOI: 10.1016/j.chc.2011.01.005.

McCart, Michael R., Paul E. Priester, W. Hobart Davies, and Razia Azen. 'Differential Effectiveness of Behavioral Parent-Training and Cognitive-Behavioral Therapy for Antisocial Youth: A Meta-Analysis.' *Journal of Abnormal Child Psychology* 34 (2006): 525–541. DOI: 10.1007/s10802-006-9031-1.

Min, Meeyoung, Kathleen Farkas, Sonia Minnes, and Lynn T. Singer. 'Impact of Childhood Abuse and Neglect on Substance Abuse and Psychological Distress in Adulthood.' *Journal of Traumatic Stress* 20, no. 5 (2007): 833–844. DOI: 10.1002/jts.20250.

Oliva, A. 'Attachment in Adolescence.' *Acción Psicológica* 8 (2011): 55–65. DOI: 10.5944/ap.8.2.190.

Pickhardt, Carl. *Surviving Your Child's Adolescence: How to Understand, and Even Enjoy, the Rocky Road to Independence.* John Wiley & Sons, 2013.

Plickert, Gabriele, and Heili Pals. 'Parental Anger and Trajectories of Emotional Well-Being from Adolescence to Young Adulthood.' *Journal of Research on Adolescence* 30, no. 2 (2020): 440–457. DOI: 10.1111/jora.12536.

Prelow, Hazel M., Marvella A. Bowman, and Scott R. Weaver. 'Predictors of Psychosocial Well-Being in Urban African American and European American Youth: The Role of Ecological Factors.' *Journal of Youth and Adolescence* 36 (2007): 543–553. DOI: 10.1007/s10964-006-9038-5.

Rajan, Chithra S., and Hepsi Bai Joseph. 'Self Esteem and Emotional Maturity among Adolescents.' *International Journal of Nursing Care* 7, no. 1 (2019): 27–29. DOI: 10.37506/ijonc.v7i1.7654.

Riquelme, María, Oscar F. García, and Emilia Serra. 'Psychosocial Maladjustment in Adolescence: Parental Socialization, Self-Esteem, and Substance Use.' *Anales de Psicología* 34, no. 3 (2018): 536. DOI: 10.6018/analesps.34.3.315201.

Scharp, Kristina M., and Lindsey J. Thomas. 'Family 'Bonds': Making Meaning of Parent–Child Relationships in Estrangement Narratives.' *Journal of Family Communication* 16, no. 1 (2016): 32–50. DOI: 10.1080/15267431.2015.1111215.

Selvini Palazzoli, Mara, Luigi Boscolo, Gianfranco Cecchin, and Giuliana Prata. 'Family Rituals: A Powerful Tool in Family Therapy.' *Family Process* 16, no. 4 (1977): 445–453. https://doi.org/10.1111/j.1545-5300.1977.00445.x.

Shearer, Cindy L., Ann C. Crouter, and Susan M. McHale. 'Parents' Perceptions of Changes in Mother-Child and Father-Child Relationships during Adolescence.' *Journal of Adolescent Research* 20, no. 6 (2005): 662–684. DOI: 10.1177/0743558405275086.

Smetana, J. G. 'Adolescents' and Parents' Conceptions of Parental Authority.' *Child Development* 59 (1988): 321–335. DOI: 10.1111/j.1467-8624.1988.tb01469.x. DOI: 10.1111/j.1467-8624.1988.tb01469.x.

Smetana, J. G. 'Adolescents' and Parents' Conceptions of Parental Authority.' *Child Development* 60 (1989): 1339–1352. DOI: 10.1111/j.1467-8624.1988.tb01469.x.

Smetana, Janet G., and P. Asquith. 'Adolescents' and parents' conceptions of parental authority and personal autonomy.' *Child Development* 65, no. 4 (1994): 1147–1162. DOI: 10.1111/j.1467-8624.1994.tb00809.x.

Steele, Ellen H., and Cliff McKinney. 'Emerging Adult Psychological Problems and Parenting Style: Moderation by Parent-Child Relationship Quality.' *Personality and Individual Differences* 146 (2019): 201-208. DOI: 10.1016/j.paid.2018.04.048.

Steinberg, Laurence, and Amanda Sheffield Morris. 'Adolescent Development.' *Annual Review of Psychology* 52, no. 1 (2001): 83-110. DOI: 10.1146/annurev.psych.52.1.83.

Steinberg, Laurence, and Jennifer S. Silk. 'Parenting Adolescents.' In *Handbook of Parenting*, edited by Marc H. Bornstein, 1:103-133. Lawrence Erlbaum Associates, 2002.

Svetaz, María Verónica, Diego Garcia-Huidobro, and Michele Allen. 'Parents and Family Matter: Strategies for Developing Family-Centered Adolescent Care within Primary Care Practices.' *Primary Care: Clinics in Office Practice* 41, no. 3 (2014): 489-506. DOI: 10.1016/j.pop.2014.05.004.

Townsend, John. *Boundaries with Teens: When to Say Yes, How to Say No*. Zondervan, 2009.

Twinkl.co.in. Accessed February 20, 2024. https://www.twinkl.co.in/teaching-wiki/parenting.

Vassar, Gerry. 'How Does a Parent's Anger Impact His or Her Child?' *Lakeside*, March 10, 2011. https://lakesidelink.com/blog/how-does-a-parents-anger-impact-his-or-her-child/.

Wolin, Steven J., and Larry A. Bennett. 'Family Rituals.' *Family Process* 23, no. 3 (1984): 401–420. DOI: 10.1111/j.1545-5300.1984.00401.x.

Yoon, Yesel. 'The Role of Family Routines and Rituals in the Psychological Well-being of Emerging Adults.' (2012). DOI: 10.7275/3215331.

Young, James W., and Lucy Rau Ferguson. 'Developmental Changes through Adolescence in the Spontaneous Nomination of Reference Groups as a Function of Decision Content.' *Journal of Youth and Adolescence* 8, no. 2 (1979): 239–252. DOI: 10.1007/BF02087623.

Zendarski, Nardia, Roslyn Galligan, David Coghill, Jonathan M. Payne, Cinzia R. De Luca, and Melissa Mulraney. 'The Associations between Child Irritability, Parental Distress, Parental Irritability and Family Functioning in Children Accessing Mental Health Services.' *Journal of Child and Family Studies* 32, no. 1 (2023): 288–300. DOI: 10.1007/s10826-022-02390-2.